Trails of

# CRATER LAKE

## National Park &
## Oregon Caves National Monument

# William L. Sullivan

### Crater Lake Natural History Association
### Oregon Caves Natural History Association

Navillus Press
Eugene

*The Chateau, the Oregon Caves' lodge.*

Prepared in partnership with the
**Crater Lake Natural History Association**
and **Oregon Caves Natural History Association** *www.craterlakeoregon.org*
P.O. Box 157
Crater Lake, OR 97604

Published by the
**Navillus Press** *www.oregonhiking.com*
1958 Onyx Street
Eugene, Oregon 97403

Printed in USA

Cover: Wizard Island from The Watchman. Inset: Room at Oregon Caves.
Spine: Golden-mantled ground squirrel. Back: Crater Lake Lodge and Oregon Caves entrance. Frontispiece: Crater Lake from the Devils Backbone.

**SAFETY CONSIDERATIONS**: Some of the trails in this book pass through remote country where hikers are exposed to unavoidable risks. On any hike, the weather may change suddenly. The fact that a trail is included in this book, or that it may be rated as easy, does not necessarily mean it will be safe or easy for you. Prepare yourself with proper equipment and outdoor skills and you will be able to enjoy your trip with confidence.

This book is updated regularly. Corrections are welcome. They may be sent to the author at *sullivan@efn.org* or to *www.craterlakeoregon.org*.

*Marshall Gifford proposed to Mildred Walker at Crater Lake in the summer of 1938.*

## DEDICATION

This book is dedicated to the memory of Marshall B. Gifford (1916–2009). Publication was made possible by a generous grant from his family and friends.

A Portland native, Marshall Gifford started his professional career as a purchasing agent at Crater Lake Lodge from 1935 to 1938. He credited his experience at Crater Lake for the skills that enabled him to become the Benson Hotel's purchasing agent, and later to found Gifford's Flowers, a retail florist business that still thrives today.

Always a storyteller, Marshall enjoyed sharing tales about hiking to Garfield Peak and Mt. Scott, running relay races from the lakeshore to Wizard Island, sighting the Old Man of the Lake, and welcoming visitors to Crater Lake National Park. Marshall's emotional connection to Crater Lake spanned over 80 years.

He loved the park and he loved the trails.

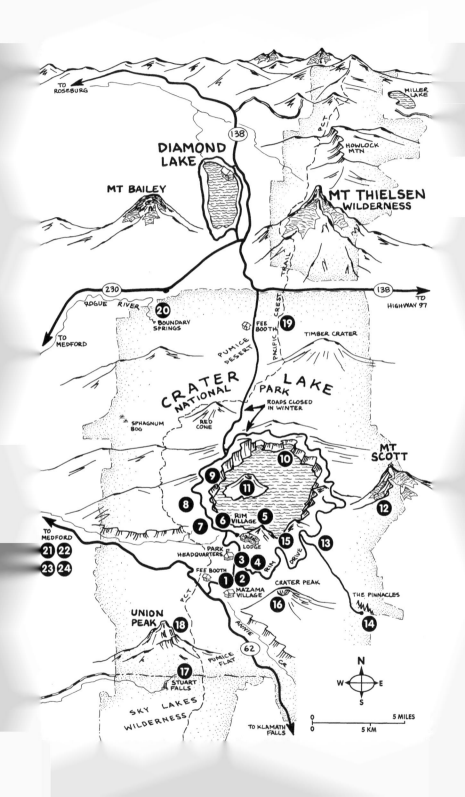

# Contents

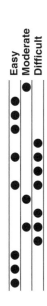

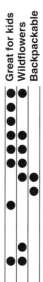

# Introduction

Welcome to the spectacular trails of Crater Lake National Park and Oregon Caves National Monument! This comprehensive guide not only has detailed maps and descriptions of every trail, but it also includes tips on where to stay and what to see during your visit to the parks. Sections on geology and history explain the stories behind the landscape. There are even color identification guides to help you identify common animals and wildflowers you may see along the way.

## HOW TO USE THIS BOOK

If you only have time for a quick visit to Crater Lake or Oregon Caves, turn to the color sections on pages 33-40 and 73-80. Here you'll find a visual tour of the parks' top attractions, as well as tips for making the most of a one- or two-day trip.

Driving directions to Crater Lake and information about lodgings and campgrounds are on page 13. Similar information for Oregon Caves is on page 92.

When planning your visit, remember that an average of 44 feet of snow fall on the Southern Oregon Cascades each winter. Snow blocks many roads and nearly all trails in Crater Lake National Park from about the start of November to mid-June. Crater Lake's popular Rim Drive typically does not open until early July, and patches of snow remain on high-elevation trails until late July. Although Oregon Caves are at a lower elevation, snow can also block trails there in winter, and cave tours are not available from the end of November to late March.

**Choose a Trail!**

Symbols in the upper right-hand corner of each trail's description make it easy to find the right kind of trip at a glance:

 Children's favorites—walks popular with the 4- to 12-year-old crowd, but fun for hikers of all ages.

 Wildflower walks—trails where you can expect the best flower displays, especially from mid-July to early August.

 Backpacking trails—routes with designated backcountry camping areas.

## Difficulty, Distance, and Elevation

To judge a hike's difficulty, pay close attention to the information blocks in the upper left-hand corner of the trail descriptions.

Hikes rated as **Easy** in this book are less than 3 miles round-trip and gain less than 500 feet in elevation. Never very steep nor remote, these short trips include several interpretive nature trails.

Hikes rated as **Moderate** range from 2 to 6 miles round-trip. These routes may gain up to 1000 feet of elevation. Hikers must be in good condition and will need to take several rest stops.

**Difficult** trails demand top physical condition, with a strong heart and strong knees. These hikes are 4 to 12 miles round-trip and may gain as much as 3000 feet. The exception to this rule is the Cleetwood Cove Trail. Because it is so heavily used, it attracts people who are unaccustomed to hiking. To warn them, this otherwise moderate trail has been rated "difficult."

**Distances** are given as the total, round-trip mileage you'll need to cover from the trailhead to the destination and back. The only trail listed with a one-way mileage is the 33.5-mile section of the Pacific Crest Trail in Crater Lake National Park.

*The popular Cleetwood Cove Trail accesses Crater Lake tour boats to Wizard Island.*

**Elevation gains** tell much about the difficulty of a hike. Those who puff climbing a few flights of stairs will find that 500 feet of elevation is a strenuous climb, and should watch this listing carefully. Note that the figures are for each hike's *cumulative* elevation gain, adding all the uphill portions, even those on the return trip.

The **hiking season** of any trail varies with the weather. In a cold year, a trail described as "Open July through October" may not yet be clear of snow by July 1, and may be socked in by a blizzard before October 31.

## RULES TO REMEMBER

### Can I Bring a Dog?

Pets are not allowed on trails, in buildings, or in backcountry areas in the National Park or National Monument. To protect the area's wildlife, dogs are allowed only on leash in developed areas such as campgrounds, picnic grounds, and parking areas. Solid excrement must be promptly removed and disposed of properly. It's best to leave pets at home.

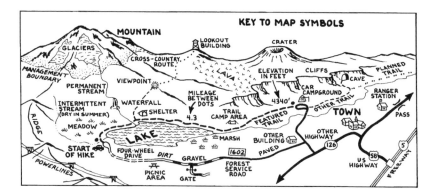

**KEY TO MAP SYMBOLS**

## Take Only Memories, Leave No Trace

Leave all rocks, plants, animals, and artifacts undisturbed for the enjoyment of future park visitors. It is not permitted, for example, to pick up a pumice rock to take home from the National Park. Do not allow children to pick flowers.

Try to leave no trace of your visit. Leave no litter. Eggshells and orange peels can last for decades.

### Don't Feed the Wildlife!

Even if cute squirrels or birds appear to be begging, offering them human food can be deadly for them and dangerous for you. These animals have plenty of seeds and other natural food far healthier for them than human food. Wild animals that become accustomed to begging lose their natural behavior, develop obesity, and are more likely to be killed by predators or winter starvation. People who feed wildlife risk being bitten, and may also be fined.

### Tips for Hikers

Please stay on designated trails, and do not shortcut switchbacks. Bicycles are allowed on only one trail described in this book, Hike #14 The Pinnacles. No trails are open to pets.

### Tips for Equestrians

Of all the trails in this book, horses and pack stock are allowed only on the Pacific Crest Trail and the section of the Lightning Springs Trail between the PCT and the designated campsites at Lightning Springs. To protect native plants, grazing is not permitted. Do not bring hay or pour grain on the ground, because this might introduce the seeds of weeds. In the National Park, horses may only be fed weed-free grain or pellets from feed bags. Horses are not allowed on trails at Oregon Caves National Monument except by special permit.

### Tips for Backpackers

Permits are required for backcountry camping in Crater Lake

*"Caveman" wedding in the Joaquin Miller Chapel of Oregon Caves in 1944. (National Park Service photo)*

National Park. They are free and can be picked up at the Rim Village Visitor Center or at the Steel Information Center at Park Headquarters on the South Entrance Road. Campfires are not allowed, so be sure to bring a backpacking stove. Designated backcountry campsites are provided at three sites along the Pacific Crest Trail and at Lightning Springs. Camping is not allowed within a mile of Rim Drive, except at Lightning Springs or in winter when the road is closed by snow. Be sure to pack out all garbage.

Seven of the trails in this book are recommended for backpackers. Use the overview map of Crater Lake National Park on pages 10-11 if you'd like to plan your own trip, connecting trails or exploring farther afield.

## SAFETY ON THE TRAIL

### Are there bears?

Grizzly bears are extinct in Oregon. The black bears that remain are smaller, generally unaggressive, and have never killed anyone in the history of Oregon. Still, these powerful animals deserve respect.

Black bears are occasionally seen in or near Crater Lake's Mazama Campground, where they have been trained by careless visitors to look for human food. If you stay in this campground, lock all food and cooler chests in the provided bear-proof boxes at night. Though bears generally avoid backcountry camps, backpackers should hang all food at least 10 feet off the ground and 5 feet from a tree trunk at night.

### Other Wild Animals

Rattlesnakes do not live in the areas described in this book. Cougars (or mountain lions) are rarely seen and have never killed anyone in Oregon's history. Cougars are nocturnal, so the only likely way you might encounter one would be if you are hiking or jogging at night. If

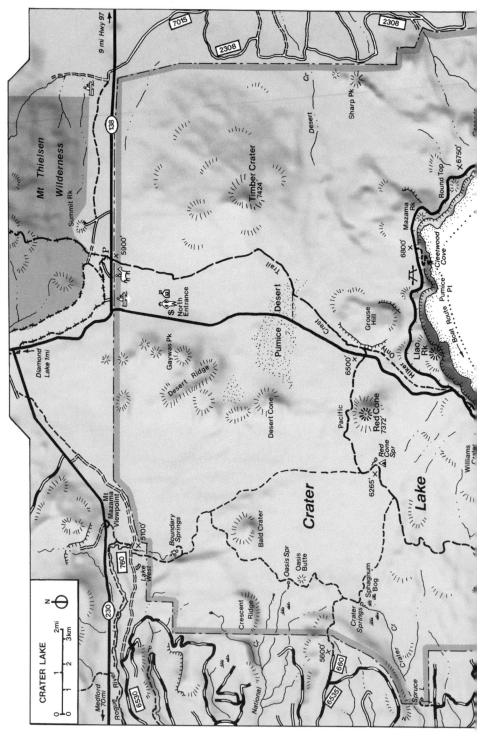

CRATER LAKE

N

0 1 2mi
0 1 2 3km

9 mi Hwy 97

7015

2308

2308

Mt Thielsen Wilderness

Summit Rk

138

Diamond Lake 1mi

P 5900'

North Entrance

Gaywas Pk

Desert Ridge

Desert Cone

Timber Crater 7424

Sharp Pk

Round Top

×6750'

Mazama Rk

6800'
×

Cleetwood Cove

Pumice Pt

Boat Route

Desert Cr

Desert Trail

Pumice Desert

Crest Trail

Grouse Hill

Llao Rk

Hiker Only

6500'
×

Pacific

Red Cone 7372

Red Cone Spr

6265'
×

Williams Crater

Crater Lake

Mt Mazama Viewpoint

×5100'

Boundary Springs

Bald Crater

Oasis Spr

Oasis Butte

Sphagnum Bog

760

Lake West

230

Crescent Ridge

National Cr

Crater Springs

Crater Cr

Medford 70mi

Rogue River

6530

5600'
×

660

6535

Spruce L

10

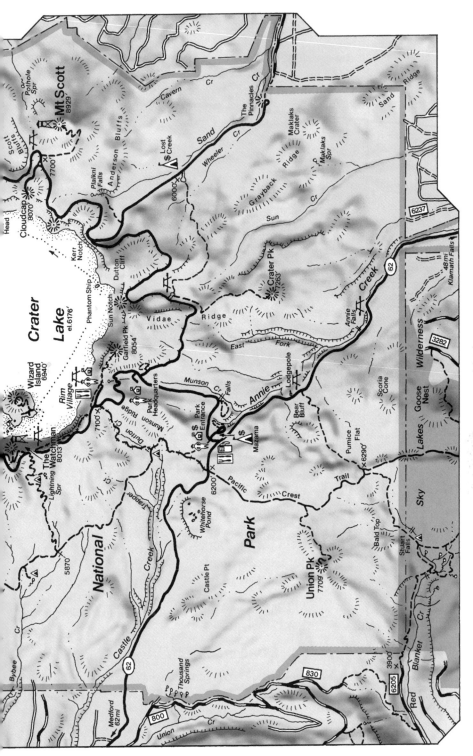

Mt Scott
8929

Scott Bluffs

Pothole Spr

Cavern Cr

The Pinnacles

Sand Cr

Cr

Sand Ridge

Maklaks Crater

Maklaks Spr

Head

Cloudcap
8070

7700'

Plaikni Falls

Anderson Bluffs

Lost Creek

6000'

Wheeler Cr

Grayback Cr

Sun

6237

Kerr Notch

Dutton Cliff

Phantom Ship

Sun Notch

Vidae

Crater Pk
7263'

Ridge

East Fork

Annie Falls

Creek

62

Crater
Lake
el.6176'

Garfield Pk
8054

Rim Village

Munson Cr Falls

Lodgepole

Scoria Cone

Wilderness

Goose Nest

3282

Klamath Falls
48mi

Wizard Island
6940

Dutton Ridge

Munson Ridge

Park Headquarters

Park Entrance

Annie

Bear Bluff

Lakes

Sky

The Watchman
8013

Lightning Spr

Trapper

6200'

Munson Cr Falls

Mazama

Pacific

Crest

Pumice Flat

6290'

Trail

Bald Top

Stuart Falls

5870

Creek

Castle

Castle Pt

Whitehorse Pond

Park

National

Union Pk
7709

Bybee Cr

62

Thousand Springs

800

Medford 62mi

Union Cr

Red Blanket Cr

3900

6205

830

11

that's what you are doing, wear a light so that you do not resemble a deer, the cougar's natural prey.

Ticks have received some publicity as carriers of Lyme disease, which begins with flu-like symptoms and an often circular rash. While this is a problem in the Eastern states, only a few cases per year have been reported in Oregon. Nonetheless, brush off your clothes and check your ankles after walking through dry grass or brush.

Mosquitoes can be a nuisance on some trails, usually in mid-July. To avoid them, remember that these insects hatch about ten days after the snow melts and that they remain in force for two or three weeks.

### Drinking Water

Day hikers should bring all the water they will need — a quart or more per person. Safe tap water is available at buildings and campgrounds. Bottled water is sold in shops and at both ends of the Cleetwood Cove Trail.

A microscopic parasite, *Giardia*, has forever changed the old custom of dipping a drink from every brook. The symptoms of "beaver fever," debilitating nausea and diarrhea, commence a week or two after ingesting *Giardia*. If you're backpacking, bring an approved water filter or purification tablet, or boil your water 5 minutes.

### Proper Equipment

On any hike a surprise storm or a wrong turn can suddenly make the gear you carry very important. It's best to bring a pack with the ten essentials: a warm, waterproof coat, drinking water, extra food, knife, matches in a waterproof container, fire starter (butane lighter or candle), first aid kit, flashlight, map, and compass. Before leaving on a backcountry trip, tell someone where you are going. If you're lost, stay put and keep warm. The number one killer in the woods is *hypothermia* — being cold and wet too long.

The maps in this book are sufficient for day hikers on most of the parks' short, well-marked trails. If you are venturing very far into the backcountry, however, you should bring a more detailed topographic map. An excellent topographic map of Crater Lake is available in the park's visitor center bookstores. Topographic maps published by the U.S. Geological Survey can be found at many outdoor stores, downloaded from the Internet for free from *msrmaps.com,* or ordered by mail from the USGS, PO Box 25286, Denver, CO 80225.

### FOR MORE INFORMATION

**Crater Lake National Park**
P.O. Box 7
Crater Lake, OR  97604
(541) 594-3000
*www.nps.gov/crla*

**Oregon Caves National Monument**
19000 Caves Highway
Cave Junction, OR  97523
(541) 592-2100 ext. 2262
*www.nps.gov/orca*

# Crater Lake National Park

Half a million people visit Oregon's National Park each year. The question visitors most often ask may well be "Why is the lake so blue?" and yes, there is an answer. But first let's look at other practical questions you may have when planning a visit—"When is the park open?" "How do I get there?" and "Where can I stay?"

## WHEN IS THE PARK OPEN?

Crater Lake National Park never closes, but because an average of 44 feet of snow fall each winter, many facilities and virtually all trails are closed from November to early June or July. The Rim Village viewpoint and the Steel Information Center at Park Headquarters are open all year.

Of the park's roads, only Highway 62 and the South Entrance Road to Rim Village are kept open in winter. Crews start plowing other roads in mid-April, clearing drifts up to 50 feet deep. West Rim Drive and the North Entrance Road from Diamond Lake typically open to traffic between late May and mid-June. East Rim Drive is the next priority, and usually opens in early July. For more information, call 541-594-3000 or check *www.nps.gov/crla.*

## HOW DO I GET THERE?

Klamath Falls, Medford, Bend/Redmond, and Eugene have the nearest commercial airports with rental cars.

If you're driving here from Interstate 5, take exit 30 in Medford and follow Crater Lake Highway 62 northeast for 76 miles. A mile beyond the Cascade summit, turn left to the park's south entrance booth. Expect to pay a $10-per-car fee here. The permits are valid for a week. Beyond the entrance booth, Mazama Village is 0.3 mile, Park Headquarters is 3.8 miles, and Rim Village is 6.4 miles.

If you're driving here from Klamath Falls, take Highway 97 north 23 miles and turn left on Highway 62 for 30 miles to the park turnoff. If you're coming from Roseburg, Eugene, or Bend, it's quickest to take the park North Entrance Road, open from about late May to September.

## WHERE CAN I STAY?

**Mazama Campground** is located near the park's south entrance booth at Mazama Village. Open from mid-June through September, the campground has 200 sites, running water, flush toilets, coin-operated showers, and laundry facilities. Expect to pay about $21 for a tent site and $27 for an RV site with an electric hookup. Half of the sites are reservable in advance at 888-774-2728. The adjacent Mazama Village has gasoline, a general store, and a buffet restaurant.

**Lost Creek Campground**, the park's only other campground, is much smaller. The 16 sites are open only to tenters on a first-come-first-served basis. Expect a $10 fee. The camp has running water and flush toilets. From Park Headquarters, take East Rim Drive counter-clockwise around the lake 8.5 miles and turn right on Pinnacles Road for 3 miles.

**Crater Lake Lodge** is a grandly renovated hotel from the early 1900s overlooking the lake at Rim Village. Usually open from mid-May to mid-October, the lodge has 71 rooms that range from about $151 to $282. Reservations should be made well in advance at 888-774-2728 or *www.craterlakelodges.com*.

**The Cabins at Mazama Village** offer 40 rooms in a less dramatic motel setting for about $126. Call 541-830-8700 for reservations.

### WHY IS THE LAKE SO BLUE?

Because the water in Crater Lake is so deep and so pure, light with long wavelengths (such as reds and yellows) penetrates deeply and is absorbed. What gets scattered back to the surface is the light with short wavelengths — the blues.

*Wizard Island from Sun Notch in April.*

*The cataclysmic eruption of Mt. Mazama, as envisioned by artist Paul Rockwood.*

# Geology of Crater Lake

The central character of Crater Lake National Park is a missing mountain. About 7700 years ago, a colossal volcanic eruption destroyed the upper half of Mt. Mazama. The resulting caldera later filled with water to become Crater Lake.

What caused the eruption? What happened during the blast? And could it happen again?

### A COLLISION IN THE EARTH'S CRUST

Mt. Mazama is just one in a string of volcanoes. The Cascade Range extends from Lassen Peak in Northern California to Mt. Garibaldi in British Columbia. It is no coincidence that these volcanoes line up roughly 100 miles inland from the Pacific shore. The mountains' fires are fueled by a collision of plates underlying North America and the Pacific seafloor.

The Earth is mostly filled with liquid rock, churned by convection currents. The surface of the Earth, by contrast, is a crust of solid rock so thin that the underlying currents have broken it up into giant, shifting plates. Continental plates are made of slightly lighter rock (mostly granite) and seafloors are made of slightly heavier rock (mostly basalt), As a result, when a continent collides with a seafloor plate, the continent tends to come out on top.

The North American plate is moving westward across the Pacific seafloor at the rate of about one inch a year. As the continent moves west, the Juan de Fuca plate of the Pacific seafloor is being *subducted* (literally,

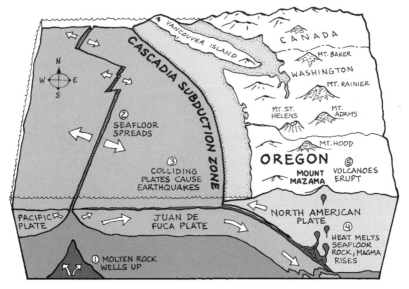

*Oregon is moving westward at the rate of about one inch a year, overriding the Pacific seafloor. When the old seafloor gets deep enough it melts rock that bubbles up as magma.*

"pulled down") beneath the advancing continent. When the subducted seafloor rock gets deep enough, the water it contains becomes so hot that it melts rock. The molten rock bubbles up to the surface, about 100 miles inland. These rising bubbles of liquid rock are the magma that fuels the volcanoes of the Cascade Range.

### THE RISE OF MOUNT MAZAMA

When rising magma creates a new volcano the runniest lava often surfaces first, building a broad, shield-shaped mountain. Mt. Mazama began perhaps 400,000 years ago as a broad mountain with a wide base. Over time Mt. Mazama added many layers of cinders and lava flows until it was perhaps 12,000 feet tall.

Volcanoes become more dangerous with age, as silica turns their magma stiff and sticky. Silica is the same mineral in window glass or beach sand. Magma rich in silica is more likely to clog a volcanic vent.

Not all silica-rich magma is violent. Sometimes it squeezes out in toothpaste fashion. Then, if it cools fast enough, it becomes obsidian, a shiny black glass. But when a vent gets clogged and pressure builds, the silica fills with gas bubbles. Then the silica blasts out as volcanic ash—tiny, abrasive shards of glass that darken the sky. Larger chunks of silica become pumice, a rock so madly frothed that it floats.

Beginning 30,000 years ago, massive flows of a stiff, silica-rich lava called dacite oozed out of Mt. Mazama's flanks. The gooey flows filled

*Phantom Ship is a lava remnant of a volcanic cone that preceeded Mt. Mazama more than 400,000 years ago, and is the oldest rock visible inside Crater Lake's caldera.*

glacial valleys with 1000 feet of gray rock, draining magma from the volcano's interior. By the time of the dacite eruptions, fireworks probably weren't shooting from the summit anymore. Instead, a broad arc of vents opened on the mountain's northern slope—the same circular crack that later became the caldera rim.

## IMAGINING THE FINAL ERUPTION

People have been living in Oregon for more than 14,000 years, so there must have been witnesses to these eruptions. Imagine that you

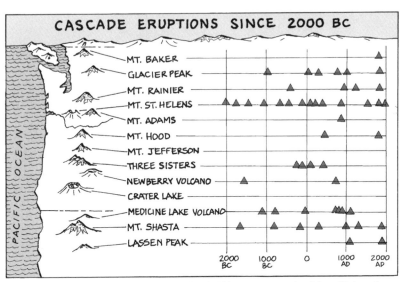

*Cascade volcanoes are fed by melted rock that bubbles up as a result of the collision of crustal plates. It's hard to know exactly when or where the next bubble will surface.*

① ASH AND PUMICE ERUPT

② CALDERA COLLAPSES

③ STEAM EXPLOSIONS

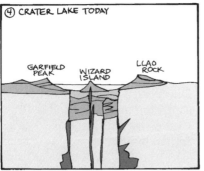

④ CRATER LAKE TODAY

GARFIELD PEAK    WIZARD ISLAND    LLAO ROCK

had been near Mt. Mazama 7700 years ago, picking huckleberries on Union Peak. From that one particularly lucky vantage point, a dozen miles southwest and upwind of the volcano, you might have survived to watch Mt. Mazama's final explosion.

Here's what you might have seen: The eruption begins when a clogged vent on Mt. Mazama's northeastern flank suddenly explodes, uncorking the volcano with a deafening boom. A mushroom cloud of pumice, ash, and rock boils 45,000 feet into the sky. Lightning crackles from hellish black clouds.

The roar continues all day, blasting twelve cubic miles of rock out of the mountain. From your viewpoint on Union Peak, you can see the ominous cloud moving downwind. What you can't see is that ten feet of fiery rock has already fallen on Klamath Marsh, twenty miles to the east. Each projectile hits the marsh with a sizzle. Nearly all of the people who live along the marsh's shore are dead.

Because of the northeast wind, the future sites of Seattle and Reno escape with just a few inches of ash, but Northeast Oregon is buried by a full foot of

*Mt. Mazama emptied its magma chamber from a side vent (1), emitted ash flows as it collapsed (2), widened and flattened the caldera floor with steam explosions (3), filled with water, and then erupted Wizard Island (4).*

grit. Even Saskatchewan is dusted with half an inch.

Before long the mountain starts to run out of steam. The initial blast has not only hollowed out the volcano, but has also fractured the surface with a gigantic, five-mile-wide spiderweb of cracks. The biggest crack circles the mountain, tracing the arc of vents on the northern flank.

Then the entire summit of Mt. Mazama slowly crumbles straight down into the emptied magma chamber.

The ground shakes and the earth roars as the mountain falls. At the same time, a fiery ring of ash starts jetting up from the perimeter of the five-mile-wide chasm. Next

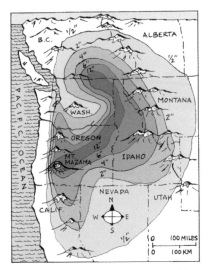

*Ashfall from Mt. Mazama's eruption fell a foot deep in Pendleton and half an inch deep as far away as Saskatchewan.*

the superheated ash spills down the mountain's flanks. From where you are standing, it looks as if a witch's cauldron has overflowed. In all directions, glowing avalanches are racing down the slopes at 70 miles an hour, incinerating trees and animals in their path.

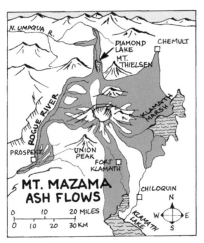

*Deadly avalanches of glowing ash raced down Mt. Mazama's slopes to Diamond Lake and the future sites of Prospect, Chemult, and Fort Klamath.*

What you are watching is a *pyroclastic flow*, a volcano's deadliest weapon. A famous pyroclastic flow from Italy's Mt. Vesuvius destroyed the Roman city of Pompeii in 79 AD, burying thousands of people with a glowing avalanche of superheated ash.

Because you are on top of Union Peak, you have some time to watch the pyroclastic flow's fiery tongue streak toward you. The deadly avalanche is just three miles away when it splits in two. One branch curves to the west, careening down the Rogue River canyon twenty miles to engulf Indian hunting camps near Prospect. The flow's other branch turns southeast, toward the villages at Klamath Lake.

Elsewhere around the ruin of Mt. Mazama, similar pyroclastic flows are fanning eastward to Klamath Marsh and Chemult. A flow to the north has rolled across Diamond Lake and is rampaging ten miles down the North Umpqua River canyon.

When the day ends, the only life visible from your lookout is a dusty stand of trees below and behind Union Peak.

## AFTER THE BLAST

Mt. Mazama's climactic blast spewed 12.2 cubic miles of rock, pumice, and ash into the atmosphere. Ice cores from Greenland glaciers show the ash layer distinctly, and narrow the date to about 5677 BC. The blast darkened the skies for up to three years and lowered the average temperature of the northern hemisphere one degree Fahrenheit.

At the mountain itself, rockslides soon widened the caldera from five miles to six. Ground water seeping into the caldera set off minor explosions, settling the debris. Then lava began oozing up. During the first 500 years after Mt. Mazama's collapse, a cubic mile of lava covered the caldera's floor.

Wizard Island emerged during these early years as well, erupting sporadically while the caldera filled with water. The other symmetrial volcanic cone on Crater Lake's floor, 1500-foot-tall Merriam Cone, never saw the light of day. It erupted entirely underwater, and remains 486 feet below the surface. Imagine the boiling water and the vast clouds of steam that must have accompanied that submarine eruption!

*Ash pinnacles at Godfrey Glen (Hike #2) remain from Mt. Mazama's pyroclastic flows.*

*With no inlet or outlet, Crater Lake maintains its level through precipitation and seepage.*

There have been no eruptions at Crater Lake for 4800 years. To be sure, warm springs on the lake bottom show there's still fire in the old mountain. But when ranking Cascade volcanoes for the likelihood of eruption in the near future, geologists more often choose South Sister, Mt. Newberry, or of course, Mt. St. Helens.

## FILLING CRATER LAKE

With a volume of more than four cubic miles, Crater Lake contains more water than all of Oregon's other lakes and reservoirs combined. The 1943-foot-deep lake has no inlet creeks, so how could it possibly have filled?

Surprisingly, enough rain and snow fall on Crater Lake that scientists estimate it took less than 740 years to fill. The only reason the caldera doesn't overflow is that the low, northern rim has a layer of permeable rock where water leaks out. The water probably percolates through the ground to feed springs lower on Mt. Mazama's slopes, although this remains unproven.

Shelves eroded by waves around Crater Lake's shore show that the surface level has been nearly constant for a long time.

*Native tribes met at Huckleberry Mountain, west of Crater Lake, to gather huckleberries in summer (Hescock Family Collection, Image courtesy CRLA Museum & Archive Collections).*

# History of Crater Lake

As a National Park, Crater Lake has seen more than a century of development and change. But the human story here begins many thousands of years before the park was designated in 1902.

### THE FIRST AMERICANS

Excavations at the Paisley Caves, just 80 miles east of the National Park, have uncovered the earliest known evidence of humans in the Americas. In 2008 scientists announced that they had unearthed *coprolites*—dried feces—in the caves. Although the discovery of dried feces might not seem auspicious, the find has had immense scientific value. By carbon dating the coprolites, scientists at the University of Oregon and the University of Copenhagen showed that people arrived in North America at least 14,300 years ago, almost 2000 years earlier than had previously been believed. Analysis of the coprolites' DNA revealed that these early residents are ancestors of the native tribes of the Americas, and that their DNA is similar to that of people from Siberia or East Asia.

The findings mean that people were living within sight of Mt. Mazama at least 6600 years before the mountain collapsed to create Crater Lake's caldera. The same clans who watched the mountain build itself up with lava flows and finally demolish its own summit are very likely represented by the four tribes who have lived near the mountain in historic times.

Of the four tribes, only the Klamaths are still represented by a sizable population in the area—to the east of Crater Lake. Traditionally their largest villages stood on the shores of Klamath Marsh, as well as along Upper and Lower Klamath Lakes. There they ground pond lily seeds for flour, gathered tule stalks for baskets, caught salmon in the falls between the lakes, and hunted ducks in dugout canoes.

To the west, the Takelma tribe lived along the Rogue River while the Upper Umpqua tribe lived on the tributaries of the Umpqua River. These two groups relied on deer, fish, and the potato-like roots of camas flowers for food.

Perhaps the best hunters of all, the Molalla tribe ranged along the high country of the western Cascades, although their tribal legends suggest they once lived on the eastern side of the mountains.

All four tribes were likely to meet in summer, when they gathered to pick huckleberries and hunt deer in the High Cascades. Huckleberry Mountain, just west of the National Park boundary, was a popular rendezvous. Tribespeople came each August to camp, hunt, eat, play games, and tell stories.

Some of those stories dealt with Crater Lake, and the spirit powers that destroyed a mountain there long ago.

## LEGENDS OF THE LAKE

Is it possible that the Klamath tribe could have preserved the memory of Crater Lake's formation for 7700 years? Consider the impact the original eruption must have had. Mt. Mazama, a 12,000-foot volcano, had smoked sulkily for centuries. And then one day the mountain suddenly blasted more than twelve cubic miles of pumice and ash into the sky. The debris fell two hundred feet deep on the Pumice Desert, and ten feet deep at Klamath Marsh. Hundreds of people must have died. As the mountain collapsed, a glowing avalanche of pumice and superheated gas raced down the slopes at freeway speeds as far as

*According to one legend, Wizard Island is the head of a spirit-god named Llao.*

*Llao Rock, the cliff where spirit-gods battled in a Klamath tribal legend.*

forty miles, killing still more.

Those who survived may well have left an enduring taboo on the mountain. Even into the nineteenth century, only shamans and power seekers dared to visit the spirit-infested lake in the sunken summit. No one spoke idly of such a place. Decades after United States explorers and settlers had crisscrossed Oregon, the lake did not appear on maps.

Although the Klamaths seldom spoke to outsiders about Crater Lake, their own legends reveal a surprising familiarity with the formation of the lake and its cinder cone, Wizard Island. The stories involve two of their most powerful spirit-gods: the peaceful Skell, who usually took the form of a marten (a weasel relative), and the jealous Llao, angry ringleader of dangerous spirits.

The two rivals ruled from opposite mountains. Llao lived on Mt. Mazama with his horde of minions. Skell lived with a host of friends 35 miles to the east on a mountain named *Yamsay*—literally, "the home of the north wind."

In one of the Klamath legends, Llao fell in love with a beautiful maiden from the Klamath tribe. He asked for her hand. She refused. In his anger Llao resolved to wipe out the entire tribe. He blew up Mt. Mazama, raining fiery rock on the tribe's homeland at Klamath Lake. According to the legend, the only tribespeople to survive hid in the water of Klamath Lake, breathing through reeds. When the rain of fire subsided, the top of Llao's mountain was gone. The tribe had suffered great losses, but had survived.

### LLAO'S BATTLE WITH SKELL

Another Klamath story explains what happened next. From his camp beside the ruins of Mt. Mazama, Llao devised a plan to kill his rival, Skell. Llao disguised one of his ugly underlings as a beautiful girl and sent her to Skell's home at Yamsay Mountain with the instructions to seduce Skell, tear out his heart, and bring it back for Llao to eat.

The girl couldn't trick Skell, but managed to seduce Skell's friend Weasel instead. She tore out Weasel's heart and brought it back to Llao. Soon Skell came to Llao's camp at Mt. Mazama, looking for his friend's heart. In the battle that followed, the two rivals wrestled in a field near what is now Llao Rock, a 2000-foot cliff above Crater Lake.

Llao's frightened followers hid in the nearby lake. From there they could hear the terrible roars of the gods' battle. The ground shook, breaking great rocks loose from the lake cliffs. Finally all was still. Then they saw what looked like their master Llao stride victoriously to the top of the cliff overlooking the lake. They thought Llao had won the battle. But in fact, Skell had won, and had disguised himself as Llao to fool them.

Skell tore Llao's body into pieces and threw them into the lake one by one. Llao's minions gobbled them up, thinking that they were destroying Skell. But when Skell finally threw down Llao's head, the minions realized they had been tricked into eating their own master.

To this day, Llao's head is still poking out of the water of Crater Lake, where it is now known as Wizard Island.

## PUTTING CRATER LAKE ON THE MAP

Although white explorers had been traveling through Southern Oregon since Peter Skene Ogden's fur trapping expedition here in 1826, Crater Lake did not appear on maps of Oregon for another half century. The local tribes had no interest in telling visitors about a place with such power, and most of the early visitors were not looking for scenery.

It was 1853 before John Wesley Hillman, Isaac Skeeters, and a group of gold prospectors happened to reach Crater Lake's startling cliffs at what is known today as Discovery Point. They had set out from the new gold boomtown of Jacksonville in search of a legendary Lost Cabin Mine. Hillman and Skeeters wandered up to the lake's rim looking for game. When the group returned to Jacksonville with no gold, Hillman's stories of "the bluest lake I ever saw" aroused little interest.

The lake was "discovered" again in 1862, this time by a group of prospectors making their way across the mountains to Jacksonville from Eastern Oregon's new gold boomtown, Canyon City. In an

*Annie Gaines of Fort Klamath was the first white woman to touch Crater Lake's surface (Courtesy NPS, CRLA Museum and Archives Collection).*

article with the misleading title, "Head Waters of Rogue River, Blue Lake," the Jacksonville newspaper reported that the group had also climbed Union Peak, naming it for their favored side in the ongoing Civil War.

*The first photographs of Crater Lake, taken by Peter Britt of Jacksonville in 1874, helped spread the lake's fame (Southern Oregon Historical Society photo #740).*

Yet another "discovery" of the lake came in 1865, when soldiers from nearby Fort Klamath were blazing a military road across the mountains to Jacksonville. Their reports sparked the first tourist trips to Crater Lake. That fall a party from Fort Klamath descended the rim to touch the lake itself. Among these adventurers was Annie Gaines, the young woman for whom Annie Spring and Annie Creek were named.

The lake's fame began to spread after 1874, when Jacksonville photographer Peter Britt hauled hundreds of pounds of photographic equipment and glass-plate negatives to the site of what is now Rim Village. The seven photographs Britt managed to capture became most Americans' first introduction to the spectacular lake.

## AN ADVOCATE NAMED STEEL

The man who deserves the most credit for promoting Crater Lake as a National Park is William Gladstone Steel. Born in Ohio in 1854, Steel grew up in Kansas, where he said he was fascinated by a newspaper account of the discovery of Oregon's "Deep Blue Lake." When he moved to Portland with his family at the age of 18, Steel couldn't find anyone who had actually seen Oregon's mystical lake. For a time, he put the lake out of his mind.

In 1880 Steel started his own newspaper, the Albany *Herald*. The following year he took a job with the post office. By 1885 Steel was superintendent of postal carriers in Portland. Yearning for adventure, he climbed Mt. Hood. Finally he decided to launch an expedition to see Crater Lake for himself.

In the summer of 1885 Steel and his climbing buddy Johnnie Breck packed their expedition gear—including a canvas-bottomed boat. Then they took the newly opened train line from Portland to Ashland, rode a stagecoach across the mountains to Fort Klamath, and trekked to Crater Lake.

Steel wasn't the first visitor to drag a boat down to the lakeshore, paddle to Wizard Island, and climb to the cinder cone's crater. But his trip had lasting consequences. He named Llao Rock for the god of Klamath legends. He named Wizard Island for its "weird appearance." And he made a personal vow to protect the beautiful lake from private exploitation.

## CAMPAIGN FOR A NATIONAL PARK

When William Gladstone Steel returned to Portland that fall he sent nearly a thousand letters to newspapers across the country, urging that Crater Lake be preserved as a National Park. He convinced editors and postmasters throughout Oregon to circulate petitions to save the lake.

Less than five months after Steel's visit to Crater Lake, he was in Washington, DC. His intense, grass-roots lobbying effort had won the attention of President Grover Cleveland.

Cleveland was so impressed with Steel and his plan that he set aside ten townships for preservation—360 square miles of land—while the idea of a park at Crater Lake could be studied.

The next summer, in 1886, the U.S. Geological Survey asked Steel to help outfit a scientific expedition to examine the lake. Steel commissioned a Portland boatworks to build two skiffs and a 26-foot cedar rowboat, the *Cleetwood*, for

*William Gladstone Steel was a key supporter of National Park status for Crater Lake (Oregon Historical Society, courtesy CRLA Museum and Archives Collection).*

sounding the lake. A previous attempt to measure the lake's depth had run out of line after an astonishing 550 feet.

Steel shipped the boats by railroad flatcar to Ashland and freighted them by wagon to Crater Lake. There the survey crew, led by Captain Clarence Dutton, lowered the boats down the rim, rowed out into the

*Lowering a boat to Crater Lake in 1903 (Oregon Historical Society, courtesy CRLA Museum and Archives Collection).*

lake, and began spooling out lead-weighted piano wire.

The enormity of their task became clear when they reeled out nearly a *quarter mile* of line before finding a bottom. And they were still near the shore! Over the next few days they mapped the lake with 168 soundings. After each measurement they flashed mirrors to signal their position to engineers watching from a prominent rim summit—a peak later named The Watchman in honor of the event. The maximum depth recorded in the survey, 1996 feet, proved remarkably close to the lake's actual depth, calculated later by sonar as 1943 feet.

Even the lake's great depth was not yet enough to win National Park status. For 16 years the park proposal languished, delayed by economic downturns and the concerns of logging, mining, and grazing speculators. Still, Steel refused to give up his efforts to promote Crater Lake.

## GATHERING SUPPORT FOR A PARK

In 1888, hoping to make the fishless lake attractive to sportsmen, Steel hand-carried a bucket with fingerling rainbow trout 40 miles from

*Steel (second from right) helped on* The Cleetwood *during an 1886 survey of Crater Lake's depth (Oregon Historical Society, courtesy CRLA Museum and Archives Collection).*

the Rogue River to Crater Lake. The move proved to be misguided, irrevocably changing the lake's pristine ecosystem. Today park officials are still puzzling over how to remove the fish from four cubic miles of water. Fishing with bait isn't allowed because eggs and worms might introduce still more alien species. Anglers who try with artificial lures say success is spotty. No fishing license is required.

In 1890 Steel published *The Mountains of Oregon,* a book calling for creation of a national reserve for the "lake in an extinct crater." By 1893 Crater Lake was no closer to becoming a National Park, but the lobbying effort had succeeded in convincing President Cleveland to designate the Cascade Range Forest Reserve—a huge swath of land from Mt. Hood to California that later became six National Forests.

In 1894 Steel co-founded the Mazamas, a Portland mountaineering club. A mazama is a kind of mountain goat. For the group's first meeting, 155 men and 38 women convened in a snowstorm on the summit of Mt. Hood. Steel was elected club president. He suggested that the Mazamas go to Crater Lake for a summer outing.

Hundreds of campers pitched tents at what is now the site of Crater Lake Lodge for the Mazamas' outing in August 1896. With a ceremonial bottle of Crater Lake water, club members christened the ancient volcano Mt. Mazama in honor of their club. Later that summer Steel brought wilderness champion John Muir and forest advocate Gifford Pinchot to the Mazama campsite to win their support.

Congress designated park land for Yosemite in 1864, Yellowstone in 1877, and Mt. Rainier in 1898. Finally it was Oregon's turn. On May 22, 1902, President Theodore Roosevelt signed a bill creating Crater Lake National Park.

## EARLY PARK DEVELOPMENT

William Gladstone Steel was surprised and disappointed when he was not chosen superintendent of the National Park he had helped create. While the new superintendent, William Arant, set about establishing a headquarters at Annie Spring and building a road up to the rim, Steel organized the Crater Lake Improvement Association, a private company dedicated to the development of the park as a summer resort.

Many of the developments Steel championed have become popular additions to the park. He spearheaded the effort to build Crater Lake Lodge and construct an automobile loop around the lake's rim. Other proposals by Steel, however, involved commercial schemes that have been controversial at Crater Lake.

Steel's company won concession rights for automobile tour packages in the park. Steel pushed for tourist tent cities with restaurants and gift shops at scenic locations. He also argued in favor of shortcuts to bring crowds of tourists to the lake itself. He suggested an elevator from Rim

*Construction of Crater Lake Lodge began in 1909 (Courtesy NPS, CRLA Museum and Archives Collection).*

Village, considered a tunnel through the rim, and proposed a road from the lodge to a lakeshore resort near Phantom Ship.

Steel was finally appointed park superintendent in 1913. One of Steel's more popular development plans, the construction of a hotel on the rim, may be one of the reasons that his tenure as park superintendent lasted only three years. Looking at the grand old Crater Lake Lodge today, you might wonder why this elegant hotel caused Steel such trouble. The architecture is romantic and the setting unmatched.

But the lodge here was not always grand. Built from 1909-1915 for the relatively modest price of $50,000, the building opened at a ceremony during Steel's tenure as superintendent. Everyone at the ceremony could see the lodge was unfinished. Tarpaper hung on its outside walls and flimsy beaverboard separated rooms. Throughout the building, the lightweight construction obviously had not been engineered for Crater Lake's massive winter snow loads.

*Although Crater Lake Lodge was still unfinished, work began on an addition in 1922 (Courtesy NPS, CRLA Museum and Archives Collection).*

Years of makeshift maintenance and harsh winters left the building slated for demolition in the 1980s. But a public outcry pushed the National Park Service to renovate it instead. The $35 million makeover proved to be the most expensive hotel construction project in the history of Oregon. Workers had to disassemble much of the lodge, numbering each of the rocks in its walls. Then they rebuilt the hotel and reassembled the facade. The lodge reopened in

1995 with elegant woodwork in the Great Hall and a modern bath for each guestroom. The lodge had finally become the building it should have been from the first.

After losing his position as superintendent in 1916, Will Steel was given the newly created position of park magistrate. The job had few duties, but allowed the man who had helped create the park to spend summers through 1931 in the landscape he loved best.

## RENAISSANCE IN THE DEPRESSION

The Roaring Twenties and the Great Depression were boom and bust years in most of America, but at Crater Lake they were years of solid growth, with funding for important construction projects.

The Steel Information Center and most of the other historic structions at Park Headquarters were built between 1927 and 1933. Much of Rim Village was constructed in the same years, including the Sinnott Memorial Overlook, the rockwork wall along Rim Promenade, and the original cafeteria and gift shop. To the north, The Watchman's stone lookout went up in 1931-1932. Truck hoists brought rock for these projects from roadcuts and rockslides at The Watchman.

When Franklin D. Roosevelt became President in 1933 he set out to stem the deepening Depression by launching programs to create jobs. The Civilian Conservation Corps (CCC) put millions of unemployed young men to work in forests and parks across the nation. Hundreds of CCC workers were based at two different Crater Lake camps. Camp Annie Spring, in use from 1933 to 1941, later became Mazama Campground. Camp Wineglass

Civilian Conservation Corps logo.

(1934-1938) was located just north of what is now the Lost Creek Campground. The "CCC boys" built flagstone walkways, drinking fountains, and furniture still in use today.

## AN OUTDOOR LABORATORY

Scientific interest in the park as an outdoor laboratory began with a scientific study in 1883. Since then, research has led to major changes in how the park is managed.

A study in 1958 rejected the idea of stocking additional fish in the park's waters, pointing out that the practice was not economical and might in fact be endangering Crater Lake's purity.

A nationwide study published in 1963 criticized the policy of allowing bears to scavenge food from garbage dumps in National Parks. Feeding bears had been popular with tourists at Crater Lake, but radically changed the bears' natural behavior. By the 1970s, garbage had been put in bear-proof receptacles. Visitor education programs discouraged the feeding of bears, and as a result, the number of "problem" bears declined. In 2009 the park hired its first wildlife biologist. One of his first projects was a census of the park's black bears, a step toward further research.

Forest fires were fought aggressively for the first 75 years of the park's history. By the 1970s, however, scientists warned that fires were a necessary part of forest ecology. Periodic fires reduce insect infestations and eliminate the fuel loads that lead to catastrophic fires, while at the same time encouraging huckleberries, native wildflowers, and healthy new forests. In 1977 Crater Lake National Park became the first agency in Oregon to adopt a policy allowing some naturally ignited wildfires to burn in backcountry areas.

*The submarine* Deep Rover *conducted lake research in 1988 and 1989 (NPS photo).*

The lake itself has also been a subject of scientific study. Researchers in 1967 determined that the lake's famous clarity had declined by 25-30% since 1937, due to an increase in plankton. Suspicion that the plankton growth was fed by nutrients from sewage led the park to replace a Rim Village septic system in 1991.

Another lake study used a one-man submarine named *Deep Rover* to explore the lake bottom in 1988 and 1989. Researchers confirmed the presence of warm spring vents on the lake floor. This evidence of ongoing geothermal activity helped block a plan to drill geothermal wells for power generation on the park's boundary.

An ongoing research project at Crater Lake is studying the effects of climate change. Average annual snowfall in the park has decreased nearly every decade since records were first kept in 1931, from an average of 614 inches in the 1930s to just 459 inches in the 2000s.

Two indicator species struggling with the warmer weather are pikas — the "rock rabbits" that live in timberline rockslides — and whitebark pines, the iconic, twisted pines at the upper edge of timberline. Pikas are so intolerant to heat that they can die from overheating on a 78° F summer day. Whitebark pines are susceptible to the insects and blister rust that thrive in warmer weather. Other long-term monitoring projects at Crater Lake are focusing on owls, invasive weeds, and rare plants.

Research, recreation, and preservation are all part of the continuing story at Crater Lake National Park.

## A Visit to
# CRATER LAKE

Crater lake fills the caldera of Mount Mazama, a volcano that collapsed in a cataclysimic eruption about 5677 BC. Today Crater Lake is the deepest lake in North America and the purest large body of water in the world. The National Park designated here in 1902 draws half a million visitors a year.

Let's take a quick visual tour of the park's top attractions. You'll find details about driving directions on page 13, geology on page 15, history on page 22, and hiking on pages 42-90.

*Wizard Island from the Devil's Backbone (Hike #9).*

# RIM VILLAGE

Perched on the caldera's spectacular brink, Rim Village serves as a starting point for many Crater Lake visits.

## RIM VISITOR CENTER

## SINNOTT OVERLOOK

Plan your visit with advice from rangers in the Rim Visitor Center (above), open 9:30am to 5pm from June through late September. Maps and books are for sale. A cafe and gift shop (below) are across Rim Village's main parking area. (Photos this page by David Grimes)

Descend a stone staircase behind the Rim Visitor Center to find the Sinnott Memorial Overlook, a viewpoint building (top of page) with exhibits, a relief map of the park (below), and 20-minute ranger talks in summer.

*Garfield Peak rises behind the lodge.*

## CRATER LAKE LODGE

*Opened in 1915, this panoramic lodge was restored in the 1990s to preserve its grand, rustic style while providing modern facilities. Tour the Grand Hall (below), sit in a rocking chair on the terrace, or check out history exhibits on the ground floor next to the lobby (open late May to early October). If you'd like to stay in one of the 71 rooms, make reservations well in advance at 888-774-2728 or www.craterlakelodges.com.*

*Waiters offer to serve drinks and snacks to visitors in the rustic rocking chairs on the lodge's scenic stone terrace.*

*Discovery Point (Hike #6).*

*The Great Hall of Crater Lake Lodge.*

## WALKS AT RIM VILLAGE

*Stroll the paved promenade along the lake's rim for a quarter mile from the Visitor Center to the lodge. Hikers can continue on unpaved trails 1.1 mile to Discovery Point (Hike #6) or 1.5 miles up to Garfield Peak (Hike #5).*

*Crater Lake from Garfield Peak (Hike #5).*

*The Steel Information Center, built in 1932.*

## PARK HEADQUARTERS

*Open year round, the Steel Information Center at Park Headquarters has helpful rangers, an 18-minute movie, and a selection of books and gifts. Two short walks begin here. The half-mile Lady of the Woods loop visits historic park buildings along Munson Creek (Hike #3). Across the road, a 0.4-mile trail leads to the 0.4-mile Castle Crest loop (Hike #4).*

## GODFREY GLEN

*Ash pinnacles rise from Godfrey Glen (below). The one-mile viewpoint loop (Hike #2) is accessible by wheelchair.*

*Above: Stepping stones on Castle Crest wildflower loop (Hike #4). Below: Sculpture on Lady of the Woods loop (Hike #3).*

## MAZAMA VILLAGE

*Near the park's south entrance, Mazama Village has a store, a restaurant, rental cabins, a 213-site campground, showers, a laundromat, and a 1.7-mile loop trail to Annie Creek (below; Hike #1).*

36

# RIM DRIVE

One of the world's most beautiful tours, Rim Drive loops 33 miles around the shattered shell of Mount Mazama. Drive clockwise for the best views, and plan to spend two to six hours, because the route has more than 30 viewpoint pullouts and many worthwhile side trails.

*Wizard Island from Rim Drive at The Watchman (Hike #9).*

## THE WATCHMAN

*Just 4 miles from Rim Village, Rim Drive passes a notch in the rim with an aerial view of Wizard Island. The view is even better if you take a 0.8-mile trail (Hike #9) up to The Watchman's patio (below) at a historic fire lookout tower.*

## CLEETWOOD COVE

*Crater Lake's most popular path— and the only trail to the lake itself— switchbacks 1.1 mile down from Rim Drive to Cleetwood Cove (above), where boats leave hourly in summer on tours that pass Llao Rock (left) and Wizard Island (below). See Hike #10.*

*Dutton Cliff towers above Phantom Ship from the viewpoint at Sun Notch (Hike #15).*

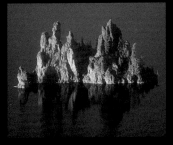

## PHANTOM SHIP

*A small, craggy island at the foot of Dutton Cliff, Phantom Ship is the 400,000-year-old remnant of a peak that predated Mount Mazama. To see the island's many moods (left), take the half-mile loop trail from Rim Drive to Sun Notch, described in Hike #15.*

## PLAIKNI FALLS

*Just a mile from Rim Drive, a new 1-mile path leads to Plaikni Falls (Hike #13). (Photos below and right by David Grimes)*

## THE PINNACLES

*Detour 6 miles from Rim Drive to a viewpoint of The Pinnacles (Hike #14).*

# A Winter Visit

Crater Lake's South Entrance Road to Rim Village is open year round, even though deep winter snows block Rim Drive and the North Entrance Road from November to June or July.

*Ski and snowshoe routes fan out from the parking area at Rim Village. The top challenge is circling the lake on 30 snowed-under miles of Rim Drive.*

*Phantom Ship from Kerr Notch in March.*

*Rangers and their vehicles line up at Park Headquarters in 1941 (Courtesy NPS, CRLA Museum and Archives Collection).*

*Grayback Park, near present-day Grayback Campground, was a popular stopover on the road to Oregon Caves in 1924 (Siskiyou National Forest photo).*

# Annie Creek

**Moderate**
**1.7-mile loop**
**200 feet** elevation loss
**Open** mid-June to mid-Nov.

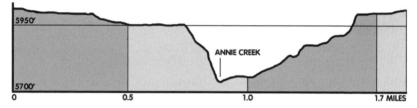

5950'

ANNIE CREEK

5700'

0          0.5          1.0          1.7 MILES

Wildflowers, tumbling brooks, and strange ash pinnacles highlight this 1.7-mile loop trail beside Crater Lake's popular Mazama Campground. Note that pets are banned on park trails.

Annie Creek honors Annie Gaines, sister-in-law of the commanding officer at nearby Fort Klamath. Annie trekked to Crater Lake, climbed down the caldera rim, and became the first woman on record to touch the lake itself on October 9, 1865.

The Annie Creek loop starts conveniently in the National Park's main campground. If you're staying in Mazama Campground, simply walk to the end of the "D" or "E" loop and follow signs to the amphitheater.

If you're driving here, head south from Rim Village 6.1 miles (or north from Highway 62 for 0.3 mile) and turn onto the Mazama Campground entrance road. Keep right and park in front of the store. Then walk through the campground to the end of camping loop D and follow signs to the amphitheater.

Behind the amphitheater, turn right on a trail that follows the wooded rim of Annie Creek's canyon along the edge of the campground. Black bears do visit these woods daily, looking for campsites with obvious cooler chests, but you're unlikely to see these unaggressive bears. On the other hand, you're almost certain to spot three species of squirrels and chipmunks. The lively, orange-bellied Douglas squirrels have no stripes and often chatter in trees. Golden-mantled ground squirrels have striped sides and scamper into burrows. Genuine chipmunks are smaller and have side stripes that extend all the way past their eyes.

*Annie Creek Trail.    Opposite: Ash formations along Annie Creek.*

After skirting the campground for 0.4 mile, the Annie Creek Trail switchbacks down into a canyon with several weird-looking ash pinnacles. The story behind the pinnacles begins in the Ice Age, when glaciers scoured U-shaped valleys through Annie Creek's canyon. After the ice retreated, the eruption of Crater Lake's Mt. Mazama filled the valley to the brim with glowing avalanches of hot pumice and ash. When the loose debris stopped moving, superheated gas rose through it, welding ash into solid rock along the vents. Since then streams have cut narrow V-shaped canyons into the softer ash, exposing the old vents as spires.

Beyond the ash pinnacles the path follows the lovely cascading stream up through wildflower meadows. Watch along the creek for water ouzels (American dippers). The ouzel looks like a dark gray robin, but by flapping its wings underwater, the ouzel is able to walk along the creek bottom for as long as two minutes, collecting insect larvae from the creekbed.

After following Annie Creek upstream for half a mile, the trail climbs back out of the canyon to complete the loop at the amphitheater.

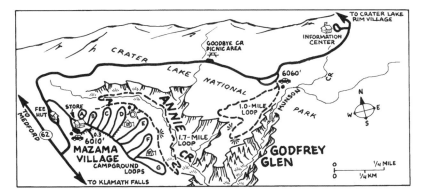

# Godfrey Glen

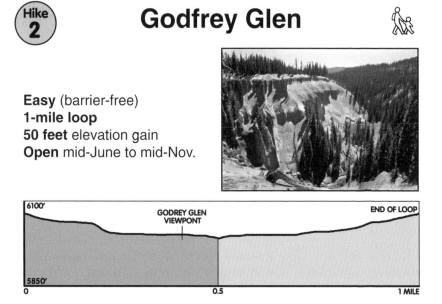

**Easy** (barrier-free)
**1-mile loop**
**50 feet** elevation gain
**Open** mid-June to mid-Nov.

6100'

GODREY GLEN
VIEWPONT

END OF LOOP

5850'

0          0.5          1 MILE

The surprise on this nearly level, wheelchair-accessible loop through the woods is a startling overlook of a beautiful canyon with strange ash pinnacles. As on all park trails, pets are not allowed.

To find the trail from the National Park's south entrance on Highway 62, drive 2.4 miles toward Rim Village and turn right at a "Godfrey Glen Nature Loop" sign for 200 yards to the trailhead. If you're coming from Rim Village, drive south 2.6 miles to Park Headquarters and continue straight another 1.4 miles to the Godfrey Glen turnoff. A trail guide booklet is available at the trailhead.

The Godfrey Glen Trail promptly forks. Keep left for the quickest route to the astonishing overlook of Godfrey Glen, a green oasis 300 feet below in a box canyon flanked by fluted spires of beige ash. If you're hiking with children, hang tight to them near this cliff-edge viewpoint.

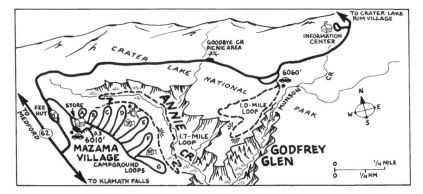

The pumice gravel here makes the lip of the cliff slippery.

What caused the pinnacles of Godfrey Glen? During the Ice Age, a glacier from Mt. Mazama filled this valley. The grinding ice widened the valley into a U-shaped canyon. After the ice retreated, the eruption of Crater Lake's Mt. Mazama filled the canyon to the brim with a glowing avalanche of hot pumice and ash. When the loose debris stopped moving, superheated gas rose through it, welding ash into solid rock along the vents. At the time, the landscape here was a vast barrens with thousands of smoking fumaroles. Since then Munson Creek has carved a V-shaped canyon through the ash. Much of the softer ash has been washed away. Where the ash was hardened by gas vents, however, pinnacles remain.

After admiring the view, continue on the loop through the forest. Although the trees are not particularly large, consider the difficulties they have overcome to grow here at all. The eruption of Mt. Mazama left this area a desert of pumice and ash. Water drains quickly from such soil, making it hard for roots to find moisture in summer. Winters, on the other hand, dump an average of 44 feet of snow here. Drifts 20 feet tall bend and bury entire trees. Despite all of this, heroic Shasta red firs and mountain hemlocks have succeeded in colonizing the area, along with a few stalwart subalpine firs and lodgepole pines.

The loop ends by returning to the junction near the parking area.

*Munson Creek from the viewpoint.     Opposite: Godfrey Glen.*

# Lady of the Woods

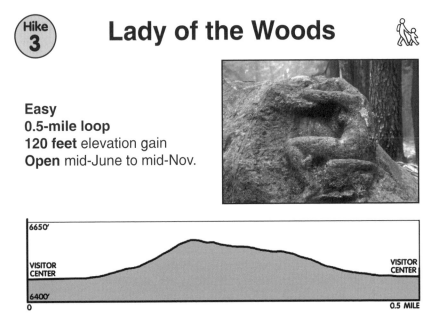

**Hike 3**

**Easy**
**0.5-mile loop**
**120 feet** elevation gain
**Open** mid-June to mid-Nov.

Elevation profile: 6650', 6400', 0 to 0.5 MILE, VISITOR CENTER (both ends)

When you stop at Crater Lake National Park's main visitor center, stretch your legs with a half-mile loop trail through the Park Headquarters' woods to see a dozen historic stone buildings designed to blend with the natural environment. Pets are not allowed on National Park trails.

If you're driving here from Highway 62, take the park's South Entrance Road 3.8 miles to Park Headquarters on the left. If you're coming from Rim Village, drive south 2.6 miles to find the headquarters. Turn into the Park Headquarters parking lot and pull up in front of the Steel Visitor Information Center. Built of massive stones and timbers in the rustic National Park style, this building opened in 1932 as a ranger dormitory. Now it's a visitor center with displays, books, brochures, and helpful rangers.

To start the loop, walk around the left-hand end of the visitor information building to the trailhead, at a footbridge over a branch of Munson Creek. A booklet describing the Lady of the Woods Loop is available here. Cross the footbridge and continue straight, heading uphill on a dirt path into the woods. To your left are a group of park maintenance buildings constructed between 1926 and 1934.

After 200 yards you'll reach a post marked #3. A doctor visiting the park in 1917 spent two weeks chiseling a reclining nude into a boulder here. Early park guides promoted the unfinished sculpture as a tourist attraction, naming it The Lady of the Woods.

Next the loop switchbacks up alongside a fork of Munson Creek in a mountain hemlock forest. At the highest point of the loop the trail crosses

46

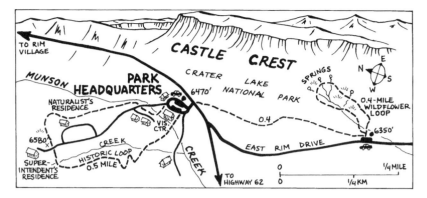

the driveway of the 1933 superintendent's residence. Designated as a national historic landmark in 1987, the impressive stone-sided residence was renovated for use as the Science and Learning Center in 2007 using funds from Oregon's Crater Lake license plate program.

At this point the path enters a creekside meadow with pink monkeyflower, purple aster, green hellebore, yellow groundsel, and views of Castle Crest's cliff.

Next the loop trail passes below the 1932 naturalist's residence. Then the path crosses a road beside a row of three identical employee residences built in consecutive years in 1927, 1928 and 1929. The loop concludes by returning to the visitor center parking lot.

*Footbridge below the 1933 superintendent's residence.    Opposite: Lady of the Woods.*

# Castle Crest

**Easy**
**0.4-mile loop**
**70 feet** elevation gain
**Open** mid-June to mid-Nov.

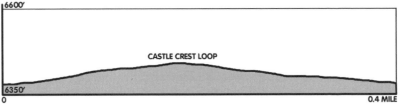

Crater Lake's showiest wildflower meadow is a slope with gushing springs at the foot of Castle Crest. An easy 0.4-mile loop tours the meadow. As on all park trails, pets and flower-picking are not allowed.

To find the trail, start at the Steel Visitor Information Center in the Park Headquarters complex, 3.8 miles north of Highway 62 or 2.6 miles south of Rim Village.

If you like, simply leave your car at the visitor center, walk to the entrance of the parking lot, cross the highway on the crosswalk, and follow a path through the trees 0.4 mile to the Castle Crest parking pullout, where the loop itself begins.

If you'd rather drive to the start of the loop, leave the visitor center parking lot, turn right for 200 yards on the highway, and fork left on

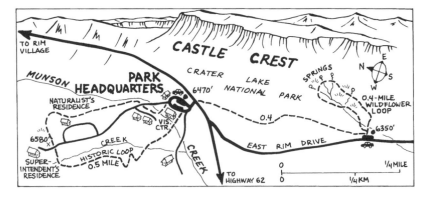

*Hummingbird (sphinx) moth.*   *Opposite: Spring crossing in the Castle Crest meadow.*

Rim Drive for 0.4 mile to a pullout on the left, just beyond a "Congested Area" sign. Trail guide booklets are available at the trailhead.

It's best to hike the loop counter-clockwise, so keep to the right. From the parking pullout, cross a footbridge over a 10-foot-wide branch of Munson Creek. Then climb through a forest of Shasta red fir to a mossy slope of springs and flowers.

The pink flowers in this wet meadow are trumpet-shaped monkey-flowers and dart-shaped shooting stars. The white ball-shaped flowers are American bistort. The blue flowers are pea-like lupines, tiny forget-me-nots, and elephantheads. The stalks of this last wildflower are clustered with scores of tiny blossoms that really do look like elephant heads.

Hummingbirds see the color red, and are attracted to the meadow's red flowers. If you're wearing a red coat or backpack, don't be surprised if one of the tiny birds zooms up to inspect you.

A special favorite of hummingbirds is scarlet gilia, whose bright red flowers have a long, slender throat shaped just right for a hummingbird's long, slender beak. The birds help the flowers by spreading pollen and are rewarded with a sugary nectar that powers the hummingbirds' high-energy flight.

Hummingbirds are off duty in the twilight of late summer evenings, but this is precisely when you might see a hummingbird moth, also known as a sphinx moth. These insects look and act so much like hummingbirds that they are often mistaken for birds. With a body nearly the size of your thumb, the odd moths hover, hum, and sip nectar from long-necked flowers with a special long proboscis.

If you need help identifying the flowers at Castle Crest, flip to the guide on pages 77-80 of this book or pick up a flower identification flier at the Steel Information Center.

After descending from the meadow, the loop trail crosses the creek twice more before returning to the parking pullout — and the 0.4-mile connector back to the visitor center.

# Garfield Peak

**Difficult**
**3.4 miles** round-trip
**1010 feet** elevation gain
**Open** mid-July through Oct.

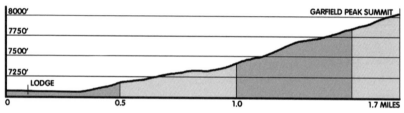

One of the prettiest trails in Crater Lake National Park follows the lake's craggy rim from the historic lodge to the wildflowers and views of Garfield Peak. As on all park trails, pets and flower-picking are banned.

The path starts from the back porch of the grand old Crater Lake Lodge. To find it, follow signs to Crater Lake's Rim Village and continue straight through this beehive of tourists 0.3 mile to a turnaround at road's end.

Truth be told, the lodge here wasn't always grand. Built from 1909-1915 at a cost of just $50,000, the building originally opened with tarpaper on its outside walls and flimsy beaverboard between rooms. Years of makeshift maintenance and harsh winters left the building slated for demolition in the 1980s. But a public outcry pushed the Park Service to

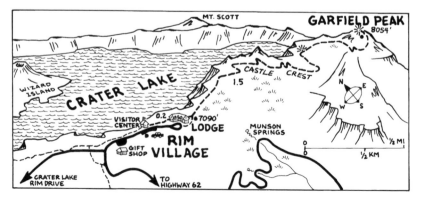

*Crater Lake from Garfield Peak.    Opposite: Garfield Peak from Crater Lake Lodge.*

renovate it instead. After a $35 million makeover, the lodge reopened in 1995 with elegant woodwork in the Great Hall, a modern bath in each guestroom, and its rustic ambiance remarkably intact.

Walk behind the lodge and turn right on the paved pathway along Crater Lake's rim. Pavement soon yields to a broad trail through meadows of pale blue lupine, bright orange paintbrush, yellow groundsel, purple daisy-shaped flea-bane, and white pearly everlasting. Views improve with each switchback. The trail climbs past cliffs of *breccia*—welded volcanic rubble from Mt. Mazama's early mountain-building eruptions. The breccia here was long buried with lava flows, but these were stripped away by glaciers before Mt. Mazama lost its summit in a cataclysmic blast about 7700 years ago.

Snow patches linger across the trail until August near the top. At this elevation, only gnarled, five-needled whitebark pines survive. These pines' limber limbs are so flexible they can be tied in knots. This helps the pines to bend rather than break in winter gales.

Garfield Peak honors the first Secretary of the Interior to visit Crater Lake. Garfield served 1907-1909 under Teddy Roosevelt, the president who created the park in 1902. When you reach the peak's summit, Crater Lake gapes below like a 4-cubic-mile pool from a high-dive tower. If you're quiet you might see foot-long marmots and guinea-pig-sized pikas watching from cliff-edge rocks 100 feet north of the summit. To the east, Mt. Scott looms above Phantom Ship, a small craggy island. To the south stretch the distant flats of Klamath Lake, with the tip of Mt. Shasta and the cone of Mt. McLoughlin to the right.

# Discovery Point

**Easy** (to Discovery Point)
**2.2 miles** round-trip
**100 feet** elevation gain
**Open** July through October

**Difficult** (to The Watchman)
**7.6 miles** round-trip
**1600 feet** elevation gain

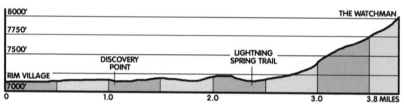

If you love the view of Crater Lake from Rim Village, but you'd rather enjoy the view without that tourist center's crowds, hike off on a quiet trail along Crater Lake's rim. For an easy walk, turn back at Discovery Point. For a tougher trek, continue along the shattered rim of ancient Mt. Mazama to a lookout tower atop The Watchman. Pets are banned on all National Park trails. If you're hiking with children, watch them carefully near the caldera's cliffs.

Start in Rim Village at the paved parking area between the gift shop and visitor center. Take the sidewalk back along Crater Lake's rim, heading clockwise around the lake. The pavement and the tourist crowds end just beyond the parking lot. After another 200 yards you'll briefly follow the shoulder of paved Rim Drive. Then the path swerves back

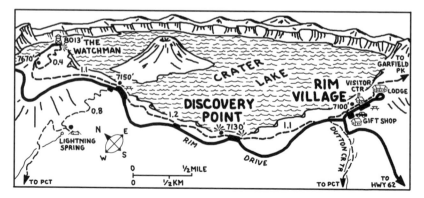

*Wizard Island from the trail in winter.    Opposite: Golden-mantled ground squirrel.*

to the caldera rim for 0.7 mile of glorious views.

The picture-postcard setting features cone-shaped Wizard Island below the massive dacite cliffs of Llao Rock, with a frame of gnarled whitebark pines and mountain hemlocks. Look for lavender cushions of five-petaled phlox along the path and raucous gray-and-black Clark's nutcrackers in the trees.

At the 1-mile mark the trail switchbacks down to cross a highway parking pullout. Then it climbs 200 yards to Discovery Point, where a bronze plaque commemorates the viewpoint from which John Wesley Hillman's prospecting party may have first spotted the lake in 1853.

For the easy hike, turn back here. If you're ready to tackle the longer trek, however, continue along the rim-edge trail. In the next 1.2 miles you'll pass two more highway parking pullouts. Then the path climbs across the shoulder of The Watchman for 1.1 mile. There are no views of the lake on this stretch, but the best view of all is coming up soon. Turn right at a junction and climb a switchbacking trail 0.4 mile to the summit's lookout tower. Here, Crater Lake suddenly opens before you, with Wizard Island seemingly at your feet.

If you've had the foresight to arrange a car shuttle to the The Watchman's trailhead, you won't even need to walk back to Rim Village. Simply descend from the Watchman 0.4 mile and turn right for another 0.4 mile down to the parking lot described in Hike #9.

# Dutton Creek

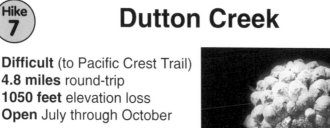

**Difficult** (to Pacific Crest Trail)
**4.8 miles** round-trip
**1050 feet** elevation loss
**Open** July through October

**Difficult** (to Lightning Spring)
**12.9-mile loop**
**1900 feet** elevation gain

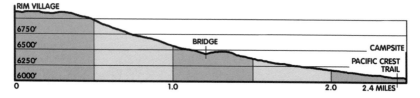

Rim Village may be the most popular destination in Crater Lake National Park, but few visitors there discover this quiet trail descending through the woods to a creekside wildflower meadow. Dutton Creek is also the closest place to Rim Village where tents are allowed, so you can backpack here too — and in that case, you might want to return on a grand 12.9-mile loop via Lightning Spring.

Day hikers should note that this trail loses over 1000 feet of elevation, so be sure to save some energy for the return trip. Backpackers need to pick up a free overnight permit in advance at a National Park office. Pets are banned on all National Park trails.

Start in Rim Village at the large paved parking area between the gift shop and visitor center. Take the paved sidewalk back along Crater Lake's rim, heading clockwise around the lake. The pavement ends just beyond the parking lot. At a junction, turn left on the Dutton Creek Trail, cross paved Rim Drive, and follow the trail downhill. At first the path parallels the road down toward Park Headquarters, but then it veers off to the right.

The next mile is a steepish descent through mountain hemlock woods. Notice the bright yellow lichen decorating tree trunks above head height. This is *Letharia* or wolf lichen. Because this lichen won't grow under snow, it serves as an indicator of the average winter snow depth.

After 1.2 miles you'll cross splashing, 6-foot-wide Dutton Creek on a footbridge. Another mile down through the woods brings you to the first of several lovely meadowed openings. Expect blue lupine, scarlet gilia, green hellebore, and chattering songbirds.

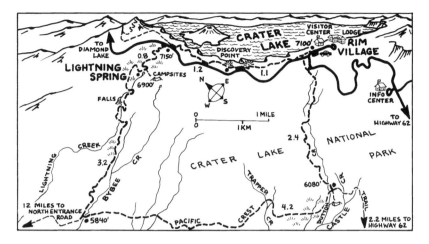

At the 2.4-mile mark you'll reach an X-shaped junction with the Pacific Crest Trail, the longest unbroken trail in the world. To the left, the PCT leads to Mexico. To the right, Canada. If you're looking for a closer goal, go straight at this junction on a short path down to Dutton Creek's designated camping area. This is a good place for a lunch stop before heading back to Rim Village.

For the longer loop, turn right (north) on the PCT. After 4.2 miles through lodgepole pine woods, turn right on the Lightning Spring Trail. This more scenic path climbs past creeks, a small meadow, and a 15-foot waterfall for 3.2 miles to Lightning Spring, where a cold, 3-foot-wide creek emerges from a dry slope.

Designated campsites near the spring are available for backpackers and equestrians. The only places in the park where horses are permitted are on the PCT and the Lightning Spring Trail up to this camp.

To continue the loop from Lightning Spring, hike a sandy trail 0.8 mile up to Rim Drive and walk 100 yards to the right along the paved road to a picnic area pullout. Here you'll find a view-packed trail that follows Crater Lake's rim 2.3 miles back to Rim Village.

*Meadow on the lower Dutton Creek Trail.     Opposite: Lodgepole pine cone.*

# Lightning Spring

**Easy** (to Lightning Spring)
**1.6 miles** round-trip
**250 feet** elevation loss
**Open** July through October

**Difficult** (to Pacific Crest Trail)
**8 miles** round-trip
**1310 feet** elevation loss

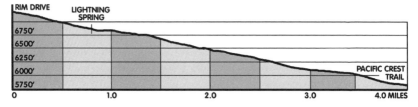

Such clear, cold water pours from Lightning Spring, high on the flank of ancient Mt. Mazama, that it almost seems as if Crater Lake has sprung a leak here. But the spring is actually much higher than the lake.

For a short walk, hike 0.8 mile down from Rim Drive to the amazing spring. For a longer hike, continue another 3.2 miles down to the Pacific Crest Trail. Just remember to save some energy for the return trip, because it's all uphill.

If you're backpacking, there are designated campsites at Lightning Spring. Be sure to pick up a free overnight permit in advance at a National Park office. Pets are banned on all National Park trails.

To find the trailhead from Rim Village, take Rim Drive north 2.5 miles. Slow down when you pass the third paved viewpoint pullout on the right. Just 100 yards later, pull into the gravel Lightning Springs trailhead on the left.

The broad trail that begins here descends a dry, sandy slope in sweeping curves. Mt. Mazama's pumice and ash fell so deep here 7700 years ago that only a few lupine, phlox, and dogbane plants have yet taken hold.

After 0.8 miles you'll reach Lightning Spring, where a deliciously cold, 3-foot-wide creek emerges from the dry slope. Campsites are nearby. Don't be surprised if you find horses hitched here. In Crater Lake National Park, horses are allowed only on the Pacific Crest Trail and on the Lightning Spring Trail up to this camp. Equestrians often tie their stock here while they walk up to the rim for a look at the lake.

If you'd like a longer hike, continue down the broad trail from the

*Creek below Lightning Spring.    Opposite: Mule deer.*

spring. The route descends a wooded valley for 3.2 miles, passing a 15-foot falls along the way. Then you'll meet the Pacific Crest Trail, the longest unbroken trail in the world. Ponder the enormity of your options here — Mexico is to the left and Canada is to the right.

If you're on a day hike, you'll have enough to do just retracing your steps 4 miles up to your car at Rim Drive. If you're backpacking, however, consider returning on a 12.9-mile loop. Turn left on the PCT for 4.2 miles to a designated camping area at Dutton Creek. Then turn left on the Dutton Creek Trail for 2.4 miles up to Rim Village, and turn left on a trail along Crater Lake's rim 2.3 miles to your car.

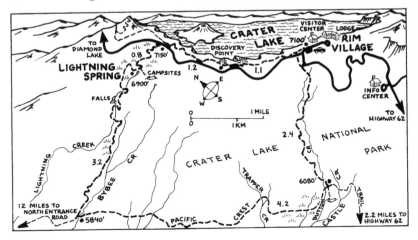

# The Watchman

Hike **9**

**Moderate** (to lookout tower)
**1.6 miles** round-trip
**413 feet** elevation gain
**Open** mid-July through Oct.

**Moderate** (to Devils Backbone)
**4 miles** round-trip
**250 feet** elevation gain

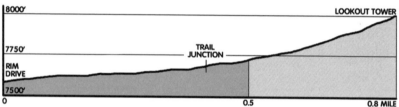

High on Crater Lake's western rim, The Watchman's lookout tower commands an eagle's-eye view across the amazingly blue lake to Wizard Island. The steep little climb up The Watchman is one of the most popular paths in the National Park. It's also short enough that you might want to extend the hike by taking an adjacent 2-mile path around Hillman Peak to a viewpoint above the Devils Backbone. Pets are banned on all park trails.

The Watchman won its name in 1886, when the U.S. Geological Survey set up a watch point here while surveyors in a boat sounded the lake with a reel of piano wire. Other names that stuck from that 1886 expedition are Cleetwood Cove (for the boat) and Dutton Cliff (for its captain). The survey recorded a maximum lake depth of 1996 feet—a

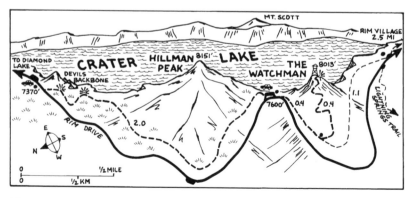

*View from the lookout tower's patio.     Opposite: The Watchman lookout.*

figure that has since been corrected by sonar to 1943 feet.

The Watchman Trail begins at a large, rail-fenced parking area and viewpoint on Crater Lake's Rim Drive. The parking area is not well marked, but you'll find it by driving 4 miles north of Rim Village or 2.2 miles south of the junction with the North Entrance Road. From the parking area, follow a paved sidewalk along the highway 100 yards to the actual trailhead. Look here for the fuzzy seedheads of western pasque flower and the blue trumpets of penstemon.

The wide path—a portion of the long-abandoned 1917 rim road— traverses a rockslide of giant cream-colored boulders. These rocks were originally part of a 50,000-year-old lava flow on Mt. Mazama's shoulder. After Mazama's cataclysmic decapitation 7700 years ago, the old lava flow was left as The Watchman, a crest on the gaping caldera's rim.

At the 0.3-mile mark, a snowfield lingers across the trail until August. Turn left at a junction just beyond the snow and climb 0.4 mile amid struggling mountain hemlock, whitebark pine, white lupine, and patches of pinkish five-petaled phlox. The summit tower, built in 1931-1932, is sometimes staffed in summer with rangers who help spot fires and answer hikers' questions. Soak in the view from the lookout's stone patio before heading back to your car.

If you'd like more exercise and different views, walk past your car and continue south up a sandy ridge to find a trail that opened in 1995. This route skirts Hillman Peak for 2 miles, passing wildflower meadows, snow patches, rockfields with cat-sized marmots, and views across the Pumice Desert to the Three Sisters.

If you can't arrange to shuttle a car to the far end of the section—a lakeview pullout 2.2 miles from The Watchman's parking lot—turn back when the trail reaches a dramatic Crater Lake viewpoint beside the Devils Backbone. This craggy wall protruding from the lake's rim is a volcanic dike, formed when magma squeezed into a vertical crack inside ancient Mt. Mazama.

# Cleetwood Cove

**Difficult**
**2.2 miles** round-trip
**700 feet** elevation loss
**Open** early July through Oct.

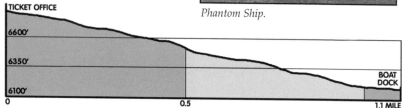

*Phantom Ship.*

The switchbacking trail down to Cleetwood Cove's tour boat dock is the most popular path in Crater Lake National Park—and the only route to the lakeshore. From there, tour boats motor past Wizard Island, Phantom Ship, and other lake landmarks. Pets are not allowed.

If you are an experienced hiker, you won't find this hike particularly difficult. But people unaccustomed to the rigors of the outdoors often stroll downhill to the lake, only to be surprised that the climb back up to their car seems hot, steep, and difficult indeed. Bring plenty of water, rest often, and take your time. Sunscreen and a hat can be important too.

To drive here from Crater Lake's Rim Village, take the Rim Drive clockwise 10.7 miles to the trailhead. If you're coming from the park's north entrance off Highway 138, turn left along the Rim Drive for 4.6 miles.

If you plan to take the boat tour, be sure to stop by the ticket trailer

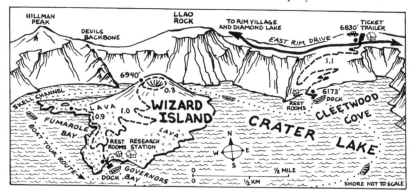

in the large parking lot across the road from the trailhead. Some reservations are now accepted for boat trips at 888-774-2728, but you still have to pick up tickets at the kiosk before hiking down.

Weather permitting, boat tours leave every 60 minutes between 10am and 3pm from early July to early September. The ticket trailer opens at 8am. On a busy summer weekend, it's not a bad idea to arrive by 9am.

A private concession company sets boat tour prices. Expect to pay about $22 for kids age 3-11 and $37 for adults ($5-$10 less if you don't get off at Wizard Island). To make sure hikers don't miss their boat, sales for each tour stop 40 minutes before it leaves.

The trail down to the boat dock is wide enough that the concessioner's lawn tractor can shuttle boat supplies on it. The route passes lodgepole pines, Shasta red firs, mountain hemlocks, manzanita bushes, and lots of glimpses down to the glowing blue lake. The amazing color results from the lake's purity (it has no inlet other than precipitation) and its 1943-foot depth (it is the deepest lake in the U.S.). In recorded history the lake has only frozen over twice and its surface level has fluctuated only 16 feet.

Gutsy swimmers sometimes brave the 50° F water at the dock's rocky shore. Fishing has been permitted without a license ever since rangers realized that introduced trout and kokanee salmon are hurting the lake's biological balance. Bait is banned, so you have to use artificial lures or flies.

The roofless tour boats carry an interpretive ranger and up to 40 passengers. It's a 45-minute ride to Wizard Island. After that the boat tour circles Phantom Ship, a small craggy island that is actually a remnant of a 400,000-year-old volcanic cone—the oldest rock exposed on the lake. On the return trip, sharp-eyed passengers sometimes spot the Old Man of the Lake, a floating vertical log that's been roaming the lake for a century.

Bring warm clothes for the sometimes chilly boat ride. And be sure to save energy for 1.1-mile climb back to your car!

*Cleetwood Cove's boat dock.*

# Wizard Island & Fumarole Bay

**Difficult** (to island crater)
**2 miles** round-trip
**760 feet** elevation gain
**Open** mid-July to mid-Sept.

**Moderate** (to Fumarole Bay)
**1.8 mile** round-trip
**150 feet** elevation gain

*Wizard Island from Fumarole Bay.*

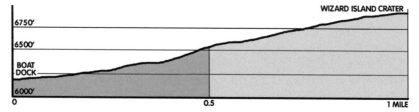

Few trails are as thrilling as those on Wizard Island, where you can climb a volcanic island inside a collapsed volcano. Only here can hikers experience Crater Lake's spectacular caldera from the inside as a 360-degree panorama.

Admittedly, getting to the trailhead is a little complicated, requiring both a prior 1.1-mile hike to the lakeshore and a ticketed boat trip across the lake. But this just makes a visit to Wizard Island all the more special.

To start, drive to the Cleetwood Cove Trailhead by taking Rim Drive clockwise around the lake 10.6 miles from Rim Village (or 4.6 miles clockwise from the North Entrance Road junction). Be sure to stop at the ticket trailer in the large parking lot across the road from the trailhead. Some advance reservations are now accepted for boat trips at 888-774-2728, but you still have to pick up tickets at the kiosk before hiking down.

Weather permitting, boat tours leave every 60 minutes between 10am and 3pm from early July to early September. The ticket trailer opens at 8am, and if you want to visit Wizard Island on a busy summer weekend, it's not a bad idea to arrive by 9am. Only the boats that leave at 9:55am and 1pm will stop at Wizard Island, and the only pickup times for the return trip are 1:45pm and 4:45pm. Overnight stays on Wizard Island are not allowed. Pets are banned on all park trails.

A private concession company sets boat tour prices. Expect to pay about $22 for kids age 3-11 and $37 for adults. To make sure hikers don't miss their boat, sales for each tour stop 40 minutes before it leaves.

Ticket in hand, hike the 1.1-mile trail down to the boat dock.

The roofless tour boats carry an interpretive ranger and up to 40 passengers. It's a 45-minute ride to Wizard Island. The island is actually one of two cinder cones that erupted from the ruins of Mt. Mazama shortly after its cataclysmic collapse 7700 years ago. The other, Merriam Cone, was left under 486 feet of water after rain and melting snow gradually filled the lake.

Wizard Island was named by Crater Lake's early promoter William Steel, who thought the cone resembled a sorcerer's hat. The trail on Wizard Island sets off through blocky black basalt lava colonized by golden-mantled ground squirrels, the red blooms of bleeding hearts, and gnarled Shasta red firs.

After just a few yards the trail forks and you face a decision. To the left, a rocky 0.4-mile side trail leads to the house-sized lava boulders and emerald lakeshore at Fumarole Bay. From there a rougher 0.5-mile path continues around the bay.

Take the right-hand fork, however, if your goal is Wizard Island's summit. This path switchbacks up the cinder cone to the top, where a 0.3-mile path circles the 90-foot-deep crater's rim. Here you'll find storm-blasted pines, red paintbrush, and often hummingbirds. If you're worried about being caught here in another volcanic eruption, relax. Although the lava and cinders here may look fresh, there have been no eruptions in the Crater Lake area for 4800 years.

Leave plenty of time to hike back to the Wizard Island dock, because there is a stiff fine if you miss the boat and they need to send another. Be sure to bring warm clothes for the return trip, because the late afternoon boat ride can be chilly. And remember to save enough energy for the 1.1-mile climb from Cleetwood Cove back to your car at Rim Drive.

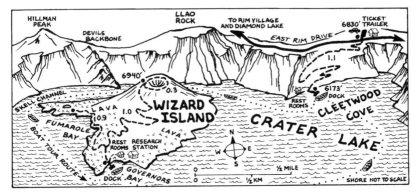

# Mount Scott

**Difficult**
**5 miles** round-trip
**1250 feet** elevation gain
**Open** mid-July to mid-Oct.

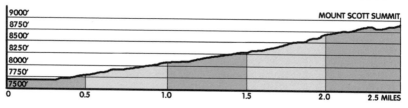

Mt. Scott's lookout tower is the only place where hikers can fit the whole breathtaking sweep of Crater Lake into an average camera viewfinder. And although this is a major mountain—the tenth tallest in Oregon's Cascades—the trail is so well-graded that even families with children sometimes tackle it.

Heavy winter snows make the Rim Drive near Mt. Scott the last road in Crater Lake National Park to open each summer. If you're driving here from Rim Village, drive south 2.8 miles toward Highway 62. Just beyond Park Headquarters, fork to the left on East Rim Drive for 11 miles to a parking pullout and trail sign on the right. If you're coming from the park's North Entrance Road, turn left on East Rim Drive for 13 miles to the trailhead. Remember that pets are banned on park trails.

The trail begins as an ancient road track amid sparse meadows and

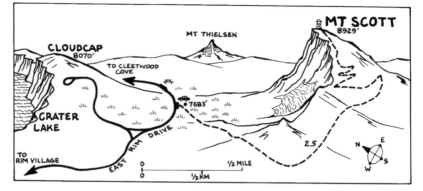

*Crater Lake from Mt. Scott.    Opposite: Mt. Scott's lookout tower.*

five-needle whitebark pines. Expect to cross a few snow patches until August. Also expect the company of Clark's nutcrackers, the cawing, gray-and-black birds that tempt visitors to defy the park's ban on feeding wildlife. In fact, these birds don't need handouts. Their sharp, strong beaks are adapted to break open whitebark pine cones for seeds, which they eat or cache for later. In return, the rugged whitebark pines, which grow only above 7000 feet, rely on the nutcrackers to spread their seeds from peak to peak.

The second mile of the trail switchbacks up a slope of pumice pebbles, strewn like ochre hailstones from Mt. Mazama's fiery storm 7700 years ago. Views open up to the south across Klamath Lake's flats to the blue silhouette of the Mountain Lakes highland and the white tip of Mt. Shasta. To the right, Mt. McLoughlin's snowy cone rises above the summits of the Sky Lakes Wilderness. Wildflowers along the way include red paintbrush, purple penstemon, and the fuzzy seed stalks of western pasque flower.

The Crater Lake panorama from the summit is breathtaking, but so is the view north to Mt. Thielsen's spire and the distant Three Sisters. Mt. Scott itself was named for Levi Scott, an 1844 Oregon Trail pioneer who founded Douglas County's Scottsburg and helped scout the Applegate Trail to Southern Oregon. The summit's two-story stone-and-frame lookout is unstaffed and closed to the public. Built in 1952, it replaced a wooden cupola-style lookout from 1917.

# Hike 13

# Plaikni Falls

**Easy** (barrier free)
**2 miles** round trip
**200 feet** elevation gain
**Open** mid-July to mid-Oct.

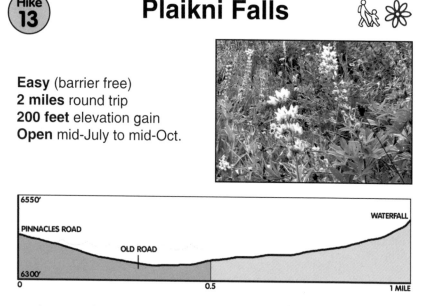

A spring-fed waterfall cascades down the cliffy face of Anderson Bluffs at the end of Crater Lake's newest trail. Set to open in September 2010, the one-mile packed gravel path is easy enough that it's accessible even to visitors in wheelchairs.

To find the trailhead from Rim Village, drive south 2.8 miles toward Highway 62. Just beyond Park Headquarters, fork to the left on East Rim Drive for 8.5 miles. Just before the Phantom Ship Overlook at Kerr Notch, turn right on Pinnacles Road. After a mile down this paved road, park at a pullout on the left. Remember that pets are banned on park trails.

The path sets off across Kerr Valley, a remarkably flat-bottomed canyon carved by one of the glaciers that descended the flanks of Mt. Mazama in the Ice Age. Rivers tend to carve V-shaped valleys, but because glaciers are so heavy and broad they excavate U-shaped valleys instead. When Mt. Mazama erupted and collapsed to create Crater Lake about 7700 years ago, the valley was amputated, leaving Kerr Notch as a U-shaped dip in the caldera rim.

As Mt. Mazama collapsed, a glowing avalanche of superheated rock and ash raced down Kerr Valley, destroying all life for miles. Since then, Shasta red fir and mountain hemlock have managed to reforest the valley. Some of the trees are hundreds of years old and as much as two feet in diameter. Because of the deep winter snow and pumice soil at this elevation, there is virtually no underbrush.

After 0.3 mile the trail crosses an abandoned roadbed, part of an old fire road to the park's eastern border. In the 1930s, this road was used

*Plaikni Falls. Opposite: Lupine by the creek. (Photos by David Grimes)*

to access a large quarry that extended to the left of the trail as far as Anderson Bluffs. Workers from the Civilian Conservation Corps (CCC) quarried rock from the cliffs to build viewpoint walkways and walls along Rim Drive. The forest is reclaiming the quarry site, although the trees there are still noticeably smaller.

The trail skirts the base of Anderson Bluffs and suddenly emerges from the woods at a meadow along Sand Creek. A few hundred feet later the trail ends at a rock-walled patio with a view of a 20-foot waterfall. Asked to choose a name for the cascade, the Klamath tribe picked *plaikni,* a Klamath word for waters from Crater Lake's high country.

Wildflowers crowding the brook here include blue lupine, pink monkeyflower, red paintbrush, and purple monkshood. To protect this fragile area, please don't leave the trail. Enjoy the wildflowers and the waterfall from the viewpoint, and then return as you came.

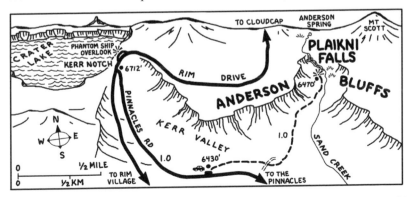

# The Pinnacles

**Easy** (to entrance monument)
**1 mile** round trip
**50 feet** elevation loss
**Open** mid-July to mid-Oct.

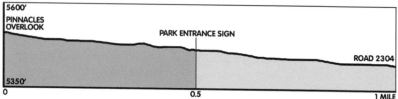

Like the spires of a lost city, pinnacles of welded ash rise from the edge of Wheeler Creek's canyon. Once this viewpoint was a stop on the east entrance road to Crater Lake National Park. Although the entrance road now ends at the viewpoint, a scenic trail continues half a mile along the canyon rim to the old park entrance monument.

From Rim Village, drive south 2.8 miles to Park Headquarters, fork to the left on East Rim Drive for 8.5 miles, and turn right on paved Pinnacles Road for 7 miles to a turnaround at road's end. Bicycles are allowed on the trail, but pets are banned.

The pinnacles here are a result of Mt. Mazama's cataclysmic eruption 7700 years ago. As the volcano collapsed, creating the caldera that later became Crater Lake, glowing avalanches of superheated ash spilled down the mountain's flanks. These high-speed pyroclastic flows are often the deadliest effect of an eruption.

Similar ash flows from Italy's Mt. Vesuvius destroyed the city of Pompei in 79 A.D., killing thousands. The pyroclastic flow here raced 30 miles to Upper Klamath Lake in about half an hour. No one knows how many people died, although Klamath legends still recall an event that nearly obliterated the tribe.

The ash flow entirely filled the canyons of Wheeler Creek and Sand Creek. For months, superheated gas continued to vent up through the ash, Thousands of smoke plumes drifted from the surface of the moonscape. Deep inside the flow, the hot gases were welding the loose ash into pillars of solid rock. Since then the creeks have eroded away most of the loose ash, exposing the hardened vents as spires.

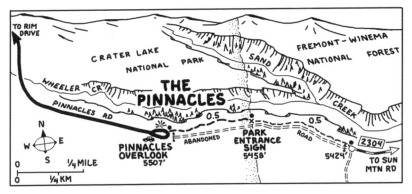

After admiring the view from the turnaround, take the trail to the right along the canyon rim. The forest here is almost entirely lodgepole pine, one of the few trees that can survive in such dry, sandy soil. It's also the only tree native to Oregon that has needles in pairs.

At the half-mile mark you'll reach a stone monument with the park's old entrance sign. Most hikers turn back here, although a fainter path with fewer views continues another half mile to a rarely used gravel turnaround at the end of Forest Service Road 2304. If you'd like to drive to this trailhead, take Highway 97 south of Diamond Lake Junction for 3 miles, turn right on Sun Mountain Road for 16 miles, and turn right on Road 2304 for 4 miles.

*The Pinnacles.    Opposite: Old park entrance monument. (Photos by David Grimes)*

# Sun Notch

**Easy**
**0.5 mile loop**
**115 feet** elevation gain
**Open** mid-July to mid-Oct.

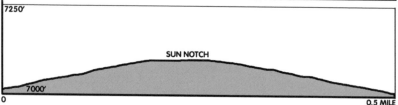

Although thousands of visitors take Rim Drive around the lake each year, most of them miss what may be the trip's best viewpoint, here at Sun Notch. It's not that the hike is difficult—the path is the length of a few city blocks—but the trailhead is deceptive. The unassuming forested slope visible from the parking area gives no hint of the spectacular vista nearby. As always on National Park trails, pets are not allowed.

If you're starting at the National Park Headquarters (halfway between Crater Lake's Rim Village and Highway 62), drive 200 yards down the road toward Highway 62, fork to the left onto East Rim Drive, and follow this road 4.3 miles to the Sun Notch Trailhead on the left.

Then hike the 0.2-mile path up through mountain hemlock woods to Sun Notch, a pass on Crater Lake's rim beside the colossal 2000-foot precipice of Dutton Cliff. Far below is Phantom Ship, a craggy little island

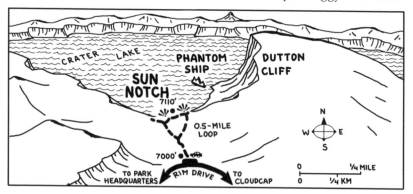

that really does resemble a ghostly steamer sailing out across Chaski Bay.

Much of Crater Lake's geologic story is exposed at this viewpoint. When eruptions started building Mt. Mazama 400,000 years ago, they began near here. Phantom Ship is a fragment of lava flows from a previous volcano at this site. It is the oldest rock visible at the lake.

As Mt. Mazama grew to an estimated height of 12,000 feet, the volcanic vents moved farther north, finally pouring out a thick dacite flow to create Llao Rock, the largest cliff visible on the opposite shore of the lake. By then, glaciers were scouring deep U-shaped valleys into the mountain's flanks. Sun Notch is a remnant of one of the largest of these glacial troughs.

The valley here at Sun Notch was amputated when the mountain exploded 7700 years ago, leaving a dip in the caldera's rim. After that cataclysmic eruption, steam explosions and rockslides quickly widened the caldera's diameter from five miles to six. Water gradually filled the hole to create the lake. A cinder cone erupted in the lake, forming Wizard Island.

Although there have been no eruptions here for 4800 years, warm springs deep beneath the lake prove there is fire in the old mountain yet.

Two paths climb from the parking lot to Sun Notch, so after you've walked the length of the notch admiring the view, you can return to your car on a loop.

*Redcloud Cliff and Sentinel Rock from Sun Notch.*     *Opposite: Phantom Ship.*

Climbing from the Ghost Room to Paradise Lost at Oregon Caves (NPS)

## A Visit to
# OREGON CAVES

Marble caverns of stalactites are the top attraction at Oregon Caves, but visitors also come away impressed by the National Monument's forest, trails, and historic buildings.

Here's a a quick visual tour of the Monument's caves, scenery, wildlife, and wildflowers. You'll find details about visitor information on page 92, geology on page 95, history on page 97, and hiking trails on pages 100-107.

Sunset from Mt. Elijah (Hike #24; photo by Lee Webb).

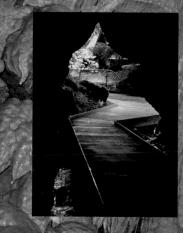

## Inside The Caves

*Most tours enter Oregon Caves near
the historic Chateau (above). A popular
90-minute tour climbs 0.6 mile, passing
Joaquin Miller's Chapel (below),
Paradise Lost (upper right), and the
Ghost Room (at right). Visitors return
on an above-ground trail to complete a
loop (National Park Service photos).*

*Joaquin Miller's Chapel.*

*A trail from Oregon Caves climbs to Mt. Elijah's summit (Lee Webb photo).*

*The lodge patio overlooks a waterfall (above). Across the street are a visitor center and bookstore (below).*

## AND ABOVE GROUND

*The Chateau (below), a 1934 lodge in the grand tradition of the National Parks, stands opposite the cave entrance. In addition to more than 20 rooms, the Chateau has a 1930s-style coffee shop, a restaurant with a mountain stream, and a historic lounge open to the public. Four hiking trails start near the Chateau. For a 3.3-mile loop, cross the street, walk through the visitor center's breeeze-way, and keep left. The loop climbs past wildflowers to Big Tree, a giant Douglas fir (Hike #23).*

*A footbridge spans Cave Creek at Grayback Campground.*

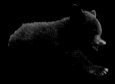

Crater Lake and Oregon Caves share many, but not all, of the species shown here and on the following four pages. Stop at the park bookstores and visitor centers for detailed checklists.

Oregon's black bears are smaller and less aggressive than grizzlies, but they do scavenge unsecured food.

A blue, a butterfly of alpine meadows.

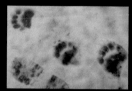

Black bear tracks in the snow.

Raccoons are occasional night visitors.

American martens hunt chipmunks and squirrels.

Bobcats are nocturnal, so people rarely see them in Oregon.

Cougars (mountain lions) are shy and nocturnal, so they are rarely seen.

Mule deer are much smaller than elk, and have large ears.

Great-horned owls roost on tree limbs by day and hunt by night.

Porcupines are slow and unaggressive, but often hurt dogs that attack them.

Elk can weigh 1000 pounds.

Pikas live in alpine rockslides.

The gray jay or "camp robber" boldly swoops to picnic tables for food scraps. Don't feed them! Human food can hurt wild animals.

Golden-mantled ground squirrels are larger than chipmunks and don't have an eye stripe.

Marmots are larger than pikas. They live in timberline rockslides and whistle when alarmed.

Townsend's chipmunk.

The Clark's nutcracker uses its bill to open whitebark pine nuts near timberline.

**ASTER** *(Aster spp.).* This purple daisy-like flower blooms late in summer, from July to September.

**POND LILY** *(Nuphar polysepalum).* Indians gathered this water plant's seeds for flour or popcorn.

**FIREWEED** *(Epilobium angustifolium).* After a fire, this plant crowds slopes with tall pink spires.

**WILD IRIS** *(Iris tenax).* Also called an Oregon flag, this June bloom varies from blue to yellowish white.

**COLUMBINE** *(Aquilegia formosa).* In wet woodlands, this bloom has nectar lobes for hummingbirds.

**FOXGLOVE** *(Digitalis purpurea).* Showy 5-foot foxglove stalks spangle sunny summer hillsides.

**PEARLY EVERLASTING** *(Anaphalis margaritacea).* These long-lasting blooms like disturbed areas.

**SOURGRASS** *(Oxalis oregana).* The shamrock-shaped leaves of sourgrass carpet forest floors.

**CANDYFLOWER** *(Claytonia sibirica).* Common by woodland creeks and trails in spring.

**WESTERN AZALEA** *(Rhododendron occidentale)* blooms in May near the Southern Oregon Coast.

**INDIAN CARTWHEEL** *(Silene hookeri).* Also called stringflower, this bloom likes dry rocky ground.

**GRASS OF PARNASSUS** *(Parnassia fimbriata).* Look for this saxifrage on grassy streambanks.

**WILD ONION** *(Allium* spp.*)*. This pungent bloom hugs the ground in dry, rocky areas.

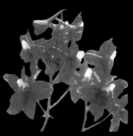

**LARKSPUR** *(Delphinium menziesii)*. Stalks of larkspur stand up to two feet tall in high meadows.

**SCARLET GILIA or SKYROCKET** *(Gilia aggregata)* blooms on dry, open slopes all summer.

**HELLEBORE or CORN LILY** *(Veratrum insolitum)* has poisonous roots and 4-foot stalks of green flowers.

**BIGELOW SNEEZEWEED** *(Helenium bigelovii)*. These bulbous blooms grow near timberline.

**MONKSHOOD** *(Aconitum columbianum)* blooms on head-high stalks in damp subalpine meadows.

**BLEEDING HEART** *(Dicentra formosa)*. Look near woodland creeks for these pink hearts.

**FRITILLARY** *(Fritillaria* spp.*)*. This odd, nodding brown "chocolate lily" likes subalpine meadows.

**SHOOTING STAR** *(Dodecatheon jeffreyi)*. Early in summer, shooting stars carpet wet fields and slopes.

**MOUNTAIN BLUEBELL** *(Mertensia* spp.*)*. A favorite browse for elk, these plants fill subalpine meadows.

**STONECROP** *(Sedum oreganum)*. This plant survives in bare, rocky ground by storing water in fat leaves.

**CONEFLOWER** *(Rudbeckia occidentalis)*. Like an odd, petalless daisy, coneflower grows waist-high.

**BUNCHBERRY** *(Cornus canadensis)*. Closely related to the dogwood tree, these small, delicate wildflowers carpet the forest floor in early summer, and the blooms develop into clusters of bright red berries in September.

**OREGON GRAPE** *(Berberis aquifolium)*. Oregon's state flower has holly-like leaves and blue berries.

**VANILLA LEAF** *(Achlys triphylla)* carpets the forest with its triple leaflets and white flower stalks.

**FAIRY SLIPPER** *(Calypso bulbosa)*. This lovely 6-inch orchid haunts the mossy floor of old-growth forests.

**PRINCE'S PINE** *(Chimaphila umbellata)*. Also known as pipsissewa, this blooms in shade.

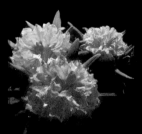

**FAIRY BELLS** *(Disporum hookeri)*. This lily of moist woodlands later develops pairs of orange berries.

**TWINFLOWER** *(Linnaea borealis)*. This double bloom grows in the far North around the globe.

**RHODODENDRON** *(Rhododendron macrophyllum)* blooms in May and can grow 20 feet tall.

**STAR-FLOWERED SOLOMONSEAL** *(Maianthemum stellata)*. These delicate stars decorate deep forests.

**LARGE SOLOMONSEAL** *(Maianthemum racemosa)*. White plumes lean across forest paths.

**TRILLIUM** *(Trillium ovatum)*. This spectacular woodland lily blooms in April, a herald of spring.

**PHLOX** *(Phlox diffusa)*. Like a colorful cushion, phlox hugs arid rock outcrops with a mat of blooms.

**PAINTBRUSH** *(Castilleja spp.)* has showy red-orange sepals, but the actual flowers are green tubes.

**PENSTEMON** *(Penstemon spp.)*. Look for these red, purple, or blue trumpets in high, rocky areas.

**ELEPHANTS HEAD** *(Pedicularis groenlandica)*. You'll see pink elephants like this in alpine bogs.

**MARSH MARIGOLD** *(Caltha biflora)*. This early bloomer likes high marshes full of snowmelt.

**AVALANCHE LILY** *(Erythronium spp.)*. These lilies erupt a week after the snow melts.

**BEARGRASS** *(Xerophyllum tenax)* resembles a giant bunchgrass until it blooms with a tall, lilied plume.

**LUPINE** *(Lupinus spp.)* has fragrant blooms in early summer and pea-pod-shaped fruit in fall.

**MONKEYFLOWER** *(Mimulus spp.)*. Clumps of these showy pink or yellow flowers line alpine brooks.

**STONECROP** *(Sedum oreganum)*. This plant survives on bare, rocky slopes by storing water in fat leaves.

**WESTERN PASQUE FLOWER** *(Anemone occidentalis)*. This high alpine flower *(left)* blooms so early it sometimes melts holes in the snow. By August it develops foot-tall, dishmop-shaped seedheads *(right)*.

The Paradise Lost formation in Oregon Caves

# Crater Peak

**Difficult**
**6.8 miles** round-trip
**1010 feet** elevation gain
**Open** mid-July to mid-Oct.

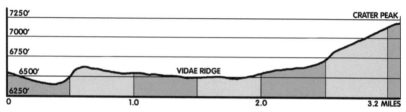

This uncrowded hike on the south side of Crater Lake reveals the difference between a crater and a caldera. Crater Lake is not really in a crater at all — it fills a *caldera*, a giant pit created by a mountain's collapse. To see a true volcanic crater, take the 3.2-mile path to Crater Peak, a cinder cone with a wildflower meadow in a cute little summit bowl. Pets are not allowed on park trails. Backpackers must bring all the water they will need and chose sites at least 100 feet from a trail.

Start at the National Park Headquarters and visitor information building located halfway between Crater Lake's Rim Village and Highway 62. Drive 200 yards down the road toward Highway 62, turn left on East Rim Drive, follow this road 2.9 miles, and turn downhill to the right to the Vidae Falls Picnic Area.

From the picnic area, the Crater Peak Trail starts out by traversing

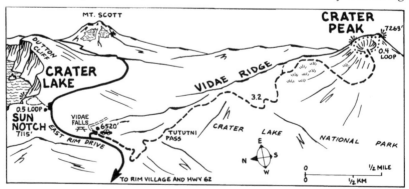

*Lupine in Crater Peak's summit meadow.    Opposite: Crater Peak from Rim Drive.*

a slope below Rim Drive for 0.6 mile. Then the path strikes off along a broad ridge through mountain hemlock woods with patches of blue lupine, scarlet gilia, and golden currant bushes.

After 2 mostly level miles the path climbs half a mile to the mouth of the summit crater. The pumice and ash that rained down from Mt. Mazama's eruption filled this little crater halfway to the top. Since then lupine, dogbane, and grass have colonized the bowl, making it a popular grazing spot for elk—look for their hoofprints and sign. A patch of snow often lingers in the crater until August.

The main trail ends at the bottom of the crater bowl. But before turning back, it's fun to take a fainter 0.4-mile loop path clockwise around Crater Peak's rim. The view-packed route around the rim is not marked, but it's hard to go astray. To the north, note Mt. Thielsen's distant spire above Sun Notch. To the east is Mt. Scott. To the west is Union Peak's spire. Look to the south to spot Klamath Lake, distant Mt. Shasta, and snowy Mt. McLoughlin.

*Crater Peak in winter, with Mt. McLoughlin on the horizon.*

# Stuart Falls

**Difficult**
**11.4 miles** round-trip
**1500 feet** elevation gain
**Open** July through October

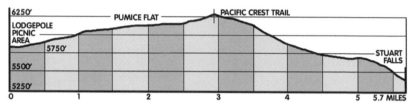

Waterfalls and huckleberries draw hikers to this canyon just outside Crater Lake National Park in the Sky Lakes Wilderness of the Rogue River - Siskiyou National Forest. To reach Stuart Falls, a 40-foot fan on a columnar basalt cliff, you have to cross Pumice Flat in the remote southern part of the park. Near the falls, both red and blue huckleberries ripen by late August. Mosquitoes can be a problem during the first three weeks of July.

If you're backpacking, permits are not required in the Sky Lakes Wilderness, but group size is limited to eight. Pets are banned on park trails.

To find the trailhead from Park Headquarters, drive 3.8 miles south to Highway 62, turn left (east) toward Klamath Falls for 3.3 miles, and park at the Lodgepole Picnic Area on the left.

To find the trailhead from the picnic area, cross Highway 62 (watching carefully for traffic!) and walk to the left along the highway shoulder a hundred yards to a small sign on the right for the Pumice Flat Trail.

The trail that begins here climbs gradually amid a forest of lodgepole pines. After a mile the path levels off to cross Pumice Flat. Underlying this two-square-mile basin is an ancient lava flow from Union Peak. The violent explosion of Mt. Mazama 7700 years ago left the flat strewn with pumice, silica-rich rock so severely frothed by volcanic gases that it can float. Despite this harsh environment, a sparse forest has managed to take hold.

At the 2.9-mile mark, on the far side of Pumice Flat, you'll reach a junction with the Pacific Crest Trail. Although you'll hardly notice that you're in a pass, this is in fact the divide between the watersheds of the Rogue and Klamath Rivers.

Turn right on the PCT for a hundred yards to another trail junction, and turn left. This path descends into the valley of Red Blanket Creek, a greener swale with mountain hemlock trees among the pines. The origin of the name Red Blanket is not certain, but may recall the wool blankets used as trading material by early settlers from the Prospect area to purchase this valley from the Takelma tribe.

Beyond the PCT crossing 2.8 miles, the roar of Stuart Falls alerts you to a short side trail to the left that leads to the waterfall's base. This makes a great lunch stop before heading back. It's also a good place to watch for water ouzels, the robin-sized dippers that can "fly" underwater.

If you are backpacking, remember that campsites should not be within 100 feet of water, so don't try to tent at the heavily used area beside the waterfall. Instead head for a less fragile camping area downstream.

*Stuart Falls.    Opposite: Shasta red fir cone.*

If you have time to explore, continue down the main trail, keeping right at junctions for 1.4 miles, to visit Red Blanket Falls, another 40-foot cascade. The route follows a delightful creek all the way.

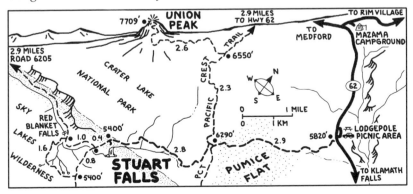

# Union Peak

**Difficult**
**11 miles** round-trip
**1600 feet** elevation gain
**Open** mid-July through October

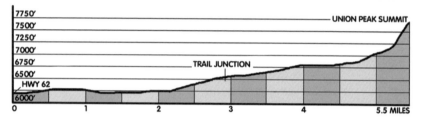

The oldest mountain in Crater Lake National Park, Union Peak's rocky volcanic plug affords a view across ancient Mt. Mazama's forested flanks to Cascade peaks from Mt. Thielsen to Mt. Shasta. The hiking route here once followed old fire roads. A new trail alignment, often wending along small forested ridges, has greatly improved the trip.

Remember that the hike ends with a steep climb up three dozen switchbacks. You'll gain nearly as much elevation in the final half mile up Union Peak as in the first five miles. A few other cautions: Backpackers must pick up an overnight permit at a National Park office, pets are not permitted, and there is no water.

From the National Park Headquarters, drive south 3.8 miles to Highway 62 and turn right toward Medford for 1 mile to the summit of Highway 62. At a "Pacific Crest Trail Parking" sign, turn south to a dirt turnaround.

The nearly level trail sets off through a sparse forest that alternates between stands of almost pure lodgepole pine and groves of almost pure mountain hemlock. The pumice that fell here several feet deep during the eruption of Crater Lake's Mt. Mazama 7700 years ago is responsible for the utter lack of underbrush.

At the 2.9-mile mark, turn right at a sign for the Union Peak Trail. The path now climbs along a small ridge. This is an area where you might see elk. Once hunted nearly to extinction, elk were restocked from Yellowstone National Park in 1917 and are thriving.

*Crater Lake's rim from Union Peak.    Opposite: Union Peak in winter.*

Suddenly the trail emerges from the woods at the base of Union Peak—a gigantic rockpile surmounted with a fortress of black crags. As you switchback up, look for the dishmop-shaped seedheads of western pasque flower and the purple trumpets of penstemon. The final short switchbacks are so rugged you may need to use your hands as you climb.

The summit's black boulders have shiny spots of melted rock where lightning has struck, proving that this is no place to be in a storm. On a clear day, however, distant Mt. Shasta floats ghost-like on the southern horizon above Devils Peak, with the cone of Mt. McLoughlin to the right. To the west is the Rogue Valley's haze. To the north, it's easy to imagine Mt. Mazama's former shape, although the mountain's forested flanks now rise to a broken hole. Crater Lake itself is hidden inside, but Llao Rock's cliff, on the lake's far shore, peeks out above Rim Village.

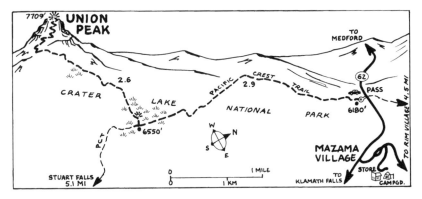

# Pacific Crest Trail

**Difficult**
**33.5 miles one way**
**2000 feet** elevation gain
**Open** July through October

*Right: Historic trail sign.*

The longest unbroken hiking trail in the world, the Pacific Crest Trail extends 2650 miles from Mexico to Canada. Conceived in 1932, designated by Congress in 1968, and officially completed in 1993, the route now attracts several hundred "through hikers" each year, who attempt to complete the entire route in one hiking season. The youngest person to accomplish this feat, 10-year-old Mary Chambers, hiked the entire PCT between April and October of 2004 with her parents.

The route was first covered on horseback in 1959. To this day, horses (but not bicycles) are allowed on the PCT. In Crater Lake National Park, where the protection of wildlife has led to many restrictions on domestic animals, equestrians are allowed only on the PCT and on the portion of the Lightning Spring Trail that leads up to a designated equestrian campsite. Hay is banned because it could introduce alien weeds. Instead,

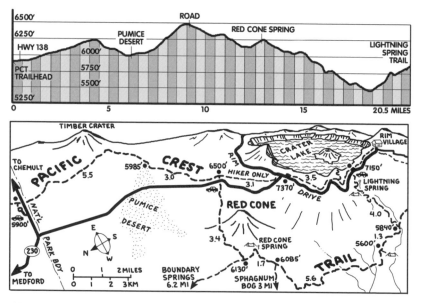

horses must be fed weed-free grain or pellets from a feed bag. PCT through hikers don't need a backcountry camping permit, but other backpackers must pick one up in advance from a National Park office.

Despite the challenge and glamour of this long-distance trail, the PCT attracts relatively few local users at Crater Lake. The trail here makes up for a lack of long-range views with old-growth woods, wildlife, small meadows, and solitude. The PCT also makes possible several interesting backpacking loops (see Hike #7) and passes three attractive backcountry camping areas.

Five trailheads access the Pacfic Crest Trail in or near the park:

- The PCT Trailhead at the summit of Highway 230. A 0.2-mile connector path leads east from this parking area to the PCT. Turn right for 0.2 mile to cross Highway 230 and enter the park.
- The Red Cone Trailhead on the park's North Entrance Road. The PCT crosses the road here. Nearby, a 3.1-mile hiker-only path allows PCT trekkers to detour up to viewpoints on the lake's rim.
- The Lightning Spring Trailhead on Rim Drive. From here a broad trail leads 0.8 mile down to a campsite and an additional 3.2 miles down to the PCT (see Hike #8).
- The PCT Trailhead at the summit of Highway 62. This is where day hikes to Union Peak (Hike #18) usually begin.
- The Pumice Flat Trailhead by the Lodgepole Picnic Area on Highway 62. A 2.9-mile hiker-only trail leads to the PCT (Hike #17).

Use the maps below (and on pages 10-11) to plan your own backcountry tour. At busy Crater Lake, the PCT can be a path to solitude.

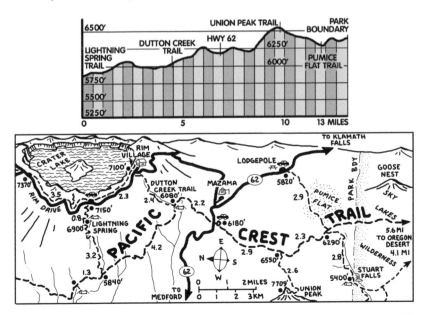

# Boundary Springs

**Moderate**
**5 miles** round-trip
**400 feet** elevation gain
**Open** June to mid-November

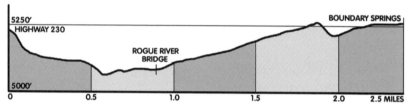

Few rivers begin as dramatically as the Rogue. At Boundary Springs, in the dry forests of Crater Lake National Park, the river pours out of the ground 20 feet wide, rushes through a meadow of yellow monkey-flowers, and tumbles over a 15-foot waterfall. Pets are banned on park trails and camping is forbidden within a quarter mile of the springs.

The headwaters of the Rogue were buried by the eruption of Crater Lake's Mt. Mazama 7700 years ago, when a glowing avalanche of hot pumice roared 40 miles downstream in a few minutes. Below Boundary Springs the river has managed to wriggle loose by carving a 100-foot-deep canyon into the vast debris field. Above the springs, snowmelt from the Crater Lake high country still has to percolate underground. The springs are not an outlet for Crater Lake itself, as was once believed.

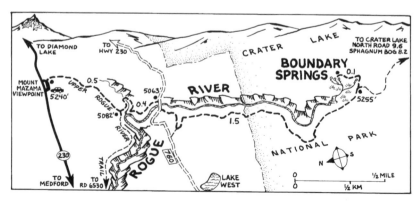

The hike to Boundary Springs starts at Mount Mazama Viewpoint, a Highway 230 pullout located 5 miles west of the junction with Highway 138 at Diamond Lake. To drive here from Medford, take Highway 62 east 57 miles and continue straight on Highway 230 toward Diamond Lake for 18.6 miles to the viewpoint on the right, between mileposts 18 and 19.

Start out on the Upper Rogue River Trail through open woods of lodgepole pine, Shasta red fir, and mountain hemlock. After half a mile turn left on the Boundary Springs Trail and begin following the Rogue River. Along the river look for robin-sized water ouzels that dip in the river, lush blue lupine (best in July), and green islands of monkeyflowers.

At the 0.9-mile mark you'll meet a dirt road. Turn right on it 100 feet to find the continuation of the trail upstream. After another 1.4 miles the trail forks at the edge of a brushy meadow. Keep left 100 yards to a 3-foot-wide spring. The trail peters out here, but don't turn back. Contour onward around a low ridge toward the sound of water 200 yards to find Boundary Springs' massive vent.

*Boundary Springs.    Opposite: Waterfall below Boundary Springs.*

*The Oregon Caves tour climbs through passages and up staircases for 0.6 mile.*

# Oregon Caves
# National Monument

Famed for its marble caverns of dripstone formations, this National Monument high in the Siskiyou Mountains also has ancient forests, historic buildings, and hiking trails. With a quaint lodge and rustic campgrounds nearby, the area warrants more than a quick trip.

### GETTING TO OREGON CAVES

If you're coming from Interstate 5, take Grants Pass exit #55 and follow "Crescent City" signs on Highway 199 for 29 miles to Cave Junction. If you're coming from the Redwoods at Crescent City, drive Highway 199 toward Grants Pass 57 miles. Once you're in Cave Junction, follow "Oregon Caves" pointers east on Highway 46 for 20 miles to the National Monument's main parking area. Unless you have room reservations at the Chateau (the park lodge), park here and walk the road 0.2 mile to the visitor center, bookstore, cave entrance, and the Chateau.

### TAKING THE CAVE TOUR

All tours through the caves are guided by rangers. The usual tour lasts 90 minutes, climbing 0.6 mile through passages and up staircases to an upper exit. From there visitors return on their own on a paved, 0.3-mile above-ground trail.

Park trails are open all year — except after severe winter snowstorms — but cave tours are offered only between late March and the end of November. From late March to the Memorial Day weekend in late May, tours leave about every hour from 10am to 4pm -- except for the last two weeks of April and throughout November, when the caves are closed Tuesday through Thursday.

In summer (from the Memorial Day weekend in late May through the Labor Day weekend in early September) cave tours leave about every half hour from 9am to 6pm. Candlelight tours are offered on many Fridays and Saturdays in summer. Guided off-trail tours are also offered, but reservations are required for these special spelunking trips; call 541-592-2100.

In fall, the standard cave tours begin about once an hour, from

The "Belly of the Whale" (NPS photo).

9am to 5pm (between the Labor Day weekend in September and early October) or from 10am to 4pm (between early October and the end of November). For current information on tour schedules, check *www.nps. gov/orca.*

Tickets for cave tours are sold only at the National Monument and only on a first-come-first-served basis. On busy summer weekends the waiting time for a tour can be as long as three hours, so it's a good idea to come before 10am when it's less crowded. Tour tickets cost about $8.50 for adults and $6 for children below age 17.

The tour route includes several steep stairways and dropoffs. Children must be at least four years old, 42 inches tall, and able to ascend and descend a set of test stairs at the visitor center to demonstrate they can complete the tour safely. Plans are in the works for rangers to lead special family tours for smaller children, perhaps by 2011.

Don't bring a flashlight or a backpack. You'll want warm clothes, however, because it's about 44° F in the cave year-round.

The Chalet's breezeway frames the Chateau.

## WHERE TO STAY

Opened in 1934, the **Chateau** at Oregon Caves National Monument ranks as a National Park Great Lodge and a National Historic Landmark. The six-story hotel has a dining room, a 1930s-era coffee shop, and more than 20 individually decorated rooms that run about $90-160 for two. The lodge is open from early May to mid-October. For reservations

check *www.oregoncaveschateau.com* or call 877-245-9022.

Two campgrounds on the highway to Oregon Caves are open from May through September. **Cave Creek Campground**, just 4 miles before the caves, has drinking water, pit toilets, and 18 campsites that run about $10. **Grayback Campground**, 8 miles before the caves, has drinking water, flush toilets, short hiking trails, and 36 campsites that run about $16-20.

*Grayback Campground has a picnic shelter and a footbridge across Cave Creek.*

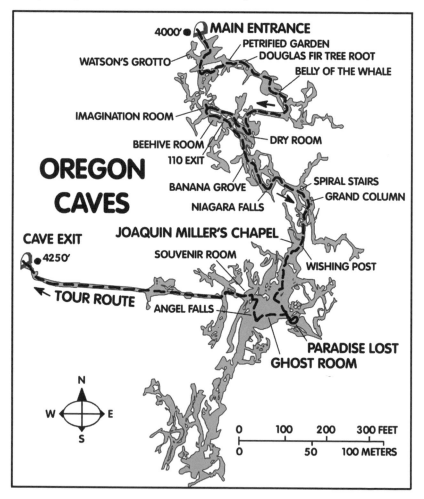

*Columns form when stalactites from the ceiling meet stalagmites from the floor, as here in the Joaquin Miller Chapel of Oregon Caves (NPS photo).*

# Geology of Oregon Caves

If you've hiked through other caves in Oregon, you've probably been in lava tubes, volcanic tunnels in recent lava flows. The marble of Oregon Caves has a much older, metamorphic origin.

The rock here began as a reef in the Pacific Ocean, perhaps as much as 250 million years ago. The calcium-rich reef eventually compacted to form limestone. Then, when the advancing North American continent scraped up this seafloor debris, the resulting pressure cooked the limestone to create marble.

The Siskiyou Mountains surrounding the caves are a jumble of at least six different *terranes* — land masses composed of islands, reefs, lava, and seafloor debris that have been rafted across the Pacific Ocean by shifting crustal plates. Originally these land masses might have resembled the islands of Japan. Because North America is moving to the northwest at the rate of about an inch a year (see graphic on page 16), terranes have been docking all along the West Coast for eons, stacking against each other like shingles on a roof.

Even on a short hike through the Siskiyous you're likely to see white and gray marble (cooked reefs), red peridotite (cooked seafloor basalt), green serpentine (metamorphosed mantle rocks), gray shale (baked seafloor mud), and speckled granitic diorite (magma that cooled slowly enough to crystallize).

Marble is hard, but water can slowly wear it away. The ground water in the Siskiyou Moluntains is acidic because bacteria in the forest soil "exhale" carbon dioxide, and water picks up the $CO_2$ to form carbonic acid. As ground water seeps through small cracks in the marble of Oregon Caves, this weak carbonic acid changes the calcite in the marble to a bicarbonate chemical that dissolves easily. Over many years, this process enlarges cracks to create the passageways of the caves.

As more calcite is dissolved, the water loses its acidity. Then, if the water hits an air pocket, the $CO_2$ bubbles off like the fizz in an opened can of soda pop. As the $CO_2$ level decreases, the water becomes less acidic and less able to hold dissolved calcium. Then each drip leaves a little calcite behind—just as a dripping faucet can stain a sink.

Drips inside the marble cave often start out by forming *soda straws*, thin tubes hanging from the ceiling. Most soda straws grow less than one inch in a thousand years. Once a tube gets plugged, water runs down the outside and forms a thicker *stalactite*. If the drip is fast, it carries dissolved calcite to the cave floor to form a *stalagmite*.

Watch for other formations as you tour Oregon Caves:

● *Columns* form when a stalctite and a stalagmite grow together, as at the Grand Column or in Joaquin Miller's Chapel.

● *Cave ghosts* are dissolved cave formations that leave white shapes on ceilings.

● *Boxwork* forms when the marble is veined with grids of resistant rock, allowing water to dissolve holes resembling post office boxes.

● *Moonmilk* is a white mix of calcite mud and bacteria with the consistency of cream cheese.

● *Cave popcorn*, a knobby calcite deposit, is caused by evaporation.

The five-acre cave system has more than three miles of passageways.

*Cave visitors at Grayback Campground in the early 1900s  (Siskiyou NF photo).*

*Oregon Caves inspired a Grants Pass booster club and mascot. (NPS photo).*

# History of Oregon Caves

Hidden on a steep, forested hillside in the Siskiyou Mountains, the entrance to Oregon Caves remained undiscovered by Euro-Americans until 1874. By then people had been living in Oregon for more than 14,000 years. When gold was found in Jacksonville in 1851, miners and ranchers began settling the surrounding valleys. The newcomers often persecuted and even murdered local Indians. After the Rogue River Indian Wars of 1853-1856, the U.S. Army rounded up the area's tribes and deported them to a reservation on the northern Oregon coast.

Elijah Jones Davidson, the cave's discoverer, was born in Illinois in 1849, but was brought to Oregon in a covered wagon as a baby. His family homesteaded near what is now southeast Portland for a few years, moved to a Willamette Valley farm near Monmouth for a decade, and then moved to Williams, a settlement 15 miles south of Grants Pass.

In 1874 Davidson wounded a deer while hunting in the forested hills a dozen miles south of Williams. His dog Bruno helped him track it down a hillside, but then Bruno vanished into a cave and "gave vent to a weird, agonizing howl." Davidson suspected the dog had found a bear.

According to an account Davidson published years later, he explored the cave in search of the bear. He lit matches to find his way through narrow passageways. When his last match died he managed to find his way out by crawling on the cave floor down a streambed until it led outside. Frustrated that he hadn't caught the bear, he left the deer carcass outside the cave as bait. Davidson bagged the bear later, after it had come out, eaten its fill, and fallen asleep.

Word of Davidson's cave spread slowly at first. Entrepreneur Walter Burch staked a claim to the cave in 1885, but never actually won ownership. He hired a crew to build a trail from the Illinois Valley, clear

a campground at the cave entrance, and install wooden ladders inside the cave. He distributed posters advertising the "Grandest Discovery of the Age: The Great LIMESTONE CAVES of Josephine County." But virtually no one came, so Burch gave up in 1888.

That same summer, William Gladstone Steel (the promoter of Crater Lake) trekked to the cave and wrote a laudatory article. Soon a new set developers, led by Alfonso Smith of San Diego, staked a claim. Smith managed to get articles about the "Oregon caves" published in the San Francisco *Examiner*. Smith boasted to reporters, outrageously, that the caves had 22 miles of passageways and 600 chambers. A horse and buggy, he lied, could be driven ten miles inside. The excitement ended in 1894, when Smith vanished and his investment company collapsed.

*About 1922, a tent camp stood at the site of what is now the Oregon Caves' visitor center (Siskiyou National Forest photo).*

In 1903 President Theodore Roosevelt set aside the caves and most of the lower Rogue River's drainage as a federal reserve — land that became the Siskiyou National Forest in 1907.

Joaquin Miller, the flamboyant "Poet of the Sierras," toured the caves in August of 1907, setting off a surge of national publicity. Less than two years later, Siskiyou National Forest Supervisor M. J. Anderson complained that the caves had been vandalized by visitors breaking off stalactites. He wrote a report recommending protection of the caves as a National Monument.

Acknowledging the need for preservation, President William H. Taft proclaimed a small 480-acre National Monument on July 12, 1909. Access remained so difficult, however, that only about 300 peple saw the new park the following year. Visitors had to struggle for days up a rough pack trail to a crude tent camp.

Things changed in 1922 when an automobile road from the Illinois Valley made access easy. Scenic buildings with rustic cedar bark siding soon replaced the caves' tent camp. A multipurpose Chalet built in 1923 serves today as a visitor center and bookstore. The Chateau, a six-story lodge, opened across the road in 1934 with a restaurant, a malt shop, more than 20 guest rooms, and rustic furniture in the National Parks tradition. Now operated by the nonprofit Illinois Valley Community Development Organization, the Chateau retains its historic charm.

Dick Rowley, a concessionaire in the 1920s, began hoking up cave tours with ghost stories and colored lights. The tradition may have helped inspire the Oregon Cavemen, a Grants Pass booster club. Members with clubs and skins posed for photographs, held meetings under "Chief Bighorn," and inducted four U.S. presidents as members.

In the 1930s young men from the Civilian Conservation Corps built many historic facilities still in use today, including trails, outbuildings, rock walls, and the Chateau's courtyard.

Over the years, "improvements" to the caves themselves have caused much damage. Workers destroyed cave formations while widening passages and building rock staircases. Heavy doors at the entrance blocked bats and other animals that had made the cave their home. The tour route was paved with asphalt in the 1950s, leaching tar into the cave's stream and discoloring dripstone with black dust. Bright fluorescent lighting encouraged moss and algae growth, turning formations green.

In 1985 the National Park Service launched a 14-year, $1.2-million restoration project to reverse the damage. Workers removed a thousand tons of rubble from earlier construction projects. The installation of bat-friendly gates allowed bats to return. Some of the broken stalactites were repaired with epoxy and powdered marble. A subtler incandescent lighting system lessened algae growth. Concrete paths of native quartz and calcite replaced asphalt.

Today the cave has a more natural look. The tour route also showcases 3000-year-old black bear bones discovered during the restoration project. Also found in the cave were 50,000-year-old

*Today the rustic Oregon Caves Chateau still looks much as it did shortly after its opening in 1934 (NPS photo).*

grizzly bear bones and the bones of a bobcat, bats, small rodents, and two jaguars—a mammal that has been extinct in Oregon for millennia.

Some historic graffiti along the tour route could not been removed. In the late 1800s, tour groups often signed their names on the dripstone in pencil. An attempt to erase those names in 1917 failed because the cave's drips had already covered the pencil marks with a thin layer of transparent calcite. Today the rock covering is even thicker, but the signatures remain—including the name of cave discoverer Elijah Davidson's brother Carter from 1878.

# Cave Tour & Cliff Nature Trail

**Easy** (cave tour)
**0.9-mile loop**
**220 feet** elevation gain
**Open** mid-March through Nov.

**Easy** (Cliff Nature Trail)
**1-mile loop**
**370 feet** elevation gain
**Open** all year

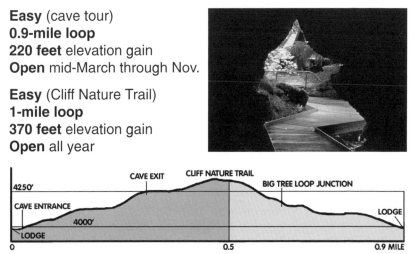

Poet Joaquin Miller's praise of the "great Marble Halls of Oregon" helped promote Oregon Caves in the years around its designation as a National Monument in 1909. Visitors today can join a guided tour for about $8.50 ($6 for children 16 and under), exploring narrow passageways and stairs to hidden rooms of cave formations. For a free hike above ground try the Cliff Nature Trail, which passes by the cave's entrance and exit. Pets are banned on all trails.

The caves' marble is mostly made of calcite, which slowly dissolves when exposed to acidic ground water. When the water loses its acidity inside the cave, it begins depositing calcite—much as a dripping faucet can stain a sink. The drips form stalactites on the ceiling, and, if the drips are fast, they also carry dissolved calcite to the cave floor to form stalagmites. To preserve the cave, the National Park Service asks strongly that visitors not touch natural features in the cave. Lighting is dim to discourage the moss and algae that grow near artificial lights.

Start your underground tour at the cave entrance near the visitor center and bookstore, 0.2 mile from the main parking lot.

Cave tours leave about every half hour from 9am to 6pm in summer, and about every hour from 10am to 4pm in spring and fall. Reservations are not accepted, so space on tours is first-come first-served. On busy summer weekends, when the wait can be as long as 3 hours, it pays to arrive early. Note that there are no tours between November 30 and mid-March, due to hibernating bats. In late April and throughout November the cave may be closed mid-week.

The tour route includes several steep stairways and dropoffs. Children must be at least four years old, 42 inches tall, and able to ascend and descend a set of test stairs at the visitor center to demonstrate they can complete the tour safely. Plans are in the works for rangers to lead special family tours for smaller children, perhaps by 2011.

Don't bring a flashlight or a backpack. You'll want warm clothes, however, because it averages about 44° F in the cave year-round.

The 90-minute tour climbs 0.6 mile through the cave to an upper exit. From there the quickest return route is a paved 0.3-mile trail to the right.

If you're going strong, however, try a slightly longer, more

*The Paradise Lost formation (National Park Service photo).    Opposite: Cave entrance.*

interesting return route. When you leave the cave exit, turn left on the Cliff Nature Trail. This path climbs to rocky vistas on a wooded bluff overlooking the distant Illinois Valley. Keep left at junctions for 0.7 mile to return along a stream to the cave entrance, completing a loop.

Even if you're not taking the cave tour, the Cliff Nature Trail makes a very nice 1-mile loop. In this case, start by walking through the visitor center's breezeway, and then keep right at junctions.

After your hike, why not celebrate with a milkshake at the Chateau's 1930s vintage malt shop?

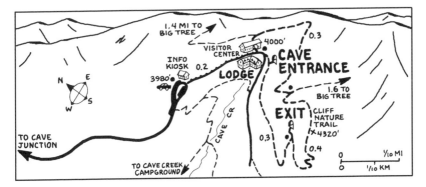

# Cave Creek & No Name Creek

**Easy** (No Name Loop)
**1.8-mile loop**
**270 feet** elevation loss
**Open** all year

**Moderate** (Cave Creek Trail)
**2.2 miles** one way
**1245 feet** elevation gain

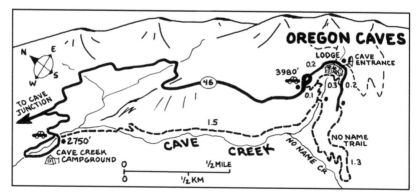

While waiting for a tour of Oregon Caves, or perhaps after tucking away lunch at the lodge, spend an hour strolling the woodsy No Name Loop. Easy enough for hikers with children, the 1.8-mile loop visits a lovely mountain stream named No Name Creek.

If you're staying at nearby Cave Creek Campground, however, you should start your hike there instead. The Cave Creek Trail leads 1.8 miles upstream to the lodge and cave entrance. Then you can return on a loop along No Name Creek. Remember that pets are not allowed on trails in Oregon Caves National Monument.

To find the trailheads from Highway 199 in Cave Junction, follow "Oregon Caves" pointers east on Highway 46. After 17 miles you'll reach the Cave Creek Campground entrance, the starting point for the Cave Creek Trail. If you'd rather start near the lodge, however, continue another 3 miles up the main highway to a turnaround. Park here and walk up the road 0.2 mile to the lodge.

To find the No Name Loop from the lodge, continue on the paved road past the cave entrance 0.2 mile to a trailhead at road's end.

The path sets off across a hillside with Douglas fir and Port Orford cedar trees. In 1934, workers mounted slabs of shaggy-barked Port Orford cedar as a rustic veneer on the Chateau, the Oregon Caves lodge.

After switchbacking down alongside No Name Creek you'll cross a footbridge to a junction with the Cave Creek Trail. Turn right for 200 yards to another trail junction. The path to the left climbs to the parking area, while the trail to the right climbs to the lodge.

These creeks are a good place to watch for a water ouzel, a dark gray, robin-sized bird that "flies" underwater in rushing mountain streams. By flapping its wings, the ouzel walks along the streambeds looking for insect larvae.

If you'd rather start your hike at Cave Creek Campground, simply follow the creekside trail upstream 1.5 miles to the No Name Loop junction. For the quickest route up to the lodge go straight 200 yards and then turn right. To return on the No Name Loop, walk past the lodge to the end of the road and take the trail that starts there.

*The Chateau, the Oregon Caves lodge.    Opposite: Water ouzel (American dipper).*

# Hike 23

# Big Tree

**Difficult**
**3.3-mile loop**
**1125 feet** elevation gain
**Open** late April through Nov.

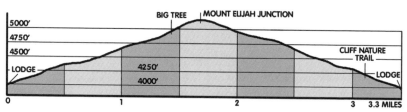

Oregon Caves National Monument has a famous cave, of course, but there's a lot to see here above ground as well. For a sampler, hike this 3.3-mile loop to wildflower meadows, rock outcrops, and one of Oregon's largest Douglas fir trees. Pets are not allowed.

Start opposite the lodge and cave entrance, next to the visitor center and bookstore. Walk through the visitor center's breezeway arch and fork to the left to find the loop trail to Big Tree. This path climbs a slope of marble outcroppings and manzanita bushes before entering an old-growth fir forest with rhododendron, vanilla leaf, and Port Orford cedar.

Expect lots of golden-mantled ground squirrels, chipmunks, and dark blue Steller's jays along this route. In wet weather you might also watch for the Oregon Cave forest snail (*Monadenia rothii*). Unique to this

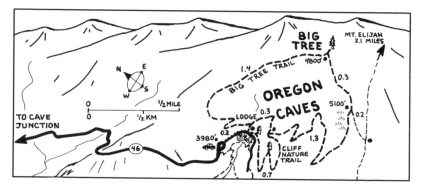

*Big Tree.    Opposite: Vanilla leaf blooming along the trail.*

area, these snails resemble reddish-brown rocks the size of golf balls. They are found nine times more often on the calcite-rich marble terrain that form the caves than on non-marble rock.

After climbing 1.4 miles you'll reach a short spur to the left that leads to Big Tree, a Douglas fir over 13 feet in diameter. It's not quite the largest Douglas fir in the world, but it's close and may yet win the crown. Currently its trunk has the largest circumference of any known Douglas fir in Oregon. It is also among the oldest Douglas firs in the world, with an estimated age of 1100 to 1200 years.

To continue, switchback up to the right and keep right at junctions. On the downhill side of this loop you'll pass high meadows of aromatic mint, orange paintbrush, purple larkspur, and cow parsnip. Finally the path descends through a grove of Port Orford cedars to return to the bookstore and visitor center by the lodge.

# Bigelow Lakes & Mt. Elijah

**Difficult** (to Mt. Elijah)
**8 miles** round trip
**2390 feet** elevation gain
**Open** mid-May to mid-Nov.

**Difficult** (to Bigelow Lakes)
**9-mile loop**
**2410 feet** elevation gain

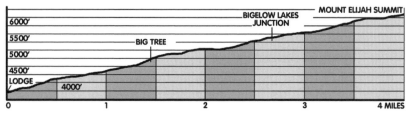

A proposed expansion of Oregon Caves National Monument would add mountain viewpoints, lakes, and challenging trails to the preserve. Sample this backcountry with a hike to a Siskiyou peak named for Elijah Davidson, discoverer of Oregon Caves. To return on a loop, descend through wildflower meadows to the Bigelow Lakes, full of lilypads.

Start at the main parking area for Oregon Caves at the end of Highway 46 from Cave Junction. Park here and walk the paved road 0.2 mile to the lodge. Turn left through a breezeway beside the gift shop/visitor center. Then fork to the left on the Big Tree loop trail.

This path climbs 1.4 miles to Big Tree, one of the state's largest Douglas fir trees. Switchback up to the right to continue. After 0.3 mile, fork

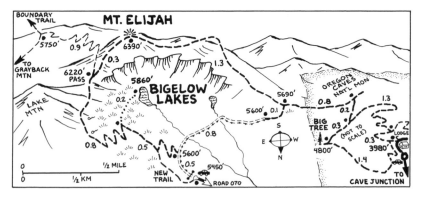

left for 0.2 mile, and then turn left on the trail to Mt. Elijah.

Follow this path up a broad ridge 2.1 miles to the the rock-strewn summit of Mt. Elijah. The view here encompasses all the Sisiyou peaks from Red Buttes (a double hump on the eastern horizon) to Preston Peak (to the south, with snow patches). Across the Illinois Valley rise the dark ridges of the Kalmiopsis Wildernesss.

You could return as you came, but for a loop continue down a ridgecrest 0.3 mile to a junction in a pass. Turn left for 0.8 mile to a switchback where the trail leaves the woods. Here a fainter path continues into the meadow straight ahead. To find the easternmost and larger of the two Bigelow Lakes, follow this side trail. Although the path soon peters out, keep crossing the meadow, heading slightly downhill to the right for 0.2 mile. The cirque lakes here host pond lilies and newts, but no fish.

After visiting the lake, return to the main trail and follow it downhill 0.5 mile to an old, abandoned portion of gravel Road 070. Turn left on the old roadbed 0.8 mile to road's end, and continue on a connector trail 0.1 mile to a ridgecrest junction. Turn right here and keep right at junctions to descend 2.6 miles back to the Oregon Caves visitor center.

There is a shortcut to Mt. Elijah if you don't mind driving gravel backroads. From the lower northeast end of the parking lot for Oregon Caves, turn uphill on gravel Road 960. Follow this steep road 2.9 miles, turn sharply right on Road 079 for 0.6 mile, and veer right on Road 070 for 0.9 to a parking area. The Forest Service is building a connector trail from here to the Bigelow Lakes, but if it's not yet finished, simply walk ahead on the barricaded roadbed half a mile, where a trail leads up to the left. Horses and dogs are allowed on these National Forest trails.

*Bigelow Lake.    Opposite: Mt.Elijah's summit.*

# Index

*Dutton Cliff and Phantom Ship from Rim Drive in winter.*

*Horse packers on the Sucker Creek Trail to Oregon Caves, circa 1920 (Siskiyou National Forest photo).*

*Launching a boat at Crater Lake in 1903 (Oregon Historical Society, courtesy CRLA Museum and Archives Collection).*

*William L. Sullivan (photo by Janell Sorensen).*

# About the Author

William L. Sullivan is the author of a dozen books and numerous articles about Oregon, including a monthly column for the Eugene *Register-Guard*. A fifth-generation Oregonian, Sullivan began hiking at the age of five and has been exploring new trails ever since. After receiving an English degree from Cornell University and studying at Germany's Heidelberg University, he completed an M.A. in German at the University of Oregon.

In 1985 Sullivan set out to investigate Oregon's wilderness on a 1,361-mile solo backpacking trek from the state's westernmost shore at Cape Blanco to Oregon's easternmost point in Hells Canyon. His journal of that two-month adventure, published as *Listening for Coyote,* was chosen by the Oregon Cultural Heritage Commission as one of Oregon's "100 Books."

Since then Sullivan has authored three novels, two books on Oregon history, and a series of *100 Hikes* guidebooks. Information about Sullivan's speaking schedule, his books, and his favorite adventures is available at *www.oregonhiking.com.*

**CRATER LAKE**
NATURAL HISTORY ASSOCIATION

Dedicated to advancing
National Park Service
educational & scientific activities

**OREGON CAVES**
NATURAL HISTORY ASSOCIATION

# About the
# Natural History Association

Established in 1942, the Crater Lake Natural History Association (CLNHA) is the officially recognized National Park Service 501 (c) (3) non-profit cooperating organization dedicated to advancing educational and scientific activities at Crater Lake National Park and Oregon Caves National Monument. The CLNHA supports Oregon Caves as the Oregon Caves Natural History Association.

### WHAT WE DO

The CLNHA prints park newspapers for Crater Lake and Oregon Caves, publishes park-related books, and purchases equipment for educational and scientific research programs requested by the Crater Lake and Oregon Caves staff.

### HOW WE DO IT

The Association operates bookstores at Crater Lake and Oregon Caves, returning profits directly to the park and monument from the sale of books, posters, maps, post cards and other interpretive materials. The bookstore at Crater Lake's Steel Information Center is open year round, the store in the Oregon Caves Visitor Center opens from late March to late November, and the bookstore at Crater Lake's Rim Village Visitor Center is open from late May to late September. These are the only stores in the parks that return profits directly to the National Park Service.

### JOIN US!

Members of the CLNHA receive newsletters, notification of events, and discounts on sale items — not only at CLNHA stores, but also at Natural History Association bookstores in most other national parks and monuments. Purchase your annual membership at a park visitor center or join online!

**Crater Lake Natural History Association**
P.O. Box 157, Crater Lake, OR 97604
541-594-3110
*www.craterlakeoregon.org*